Eating Oil
Food Supply in a
Changing Climate

Foreword

Recent large scale protests at extravagant gatherings of world leaders (Seattle, Gothenburg, Genoa) have marked a rising tide of discontent with a global economic system that is increasingly incapable of dealing with poverty, equity, social justice, environmental protection and the satisfaction of basic human needs. The lubricating oil for this global economic system is long distance transport of goods and people. In the contemporary food system, the dependency on crude oil during each stage of increasingly complicated and lengthy supply chains increases the vulnerability of food supply. This is also highly polluting and one of the consequences is climate change. Global warming is now a reality. The priority must now be to identify and adopt the options for meeting our needs that drastically reduce greenhouse gas emissions. Eating Oil shows that there is something very wrong with a global system that supplies New Zealand onions to supermarkets in the UK - and supplies them more cheaply than local sources.

The discussion about globalisation is gradually recognising the importance of celebrating what is locally distinctive (and can be supplied locally) and rejecting those things transported across the world simply to meet corporate profitability targets. *The penny has finally dropped in that we are now confronted with two very different lifestyle choices, each of which has dramatic implications for sustainable development and global equity.* Model 1 is the globalisation model and Model 2 is the localisation model.

Model 1, advocated by most leaders of the developed world and enthusiastically supported by the UK Prime Minister, Tony Blair, is of a world where most of the important decisions are made by large corporations and where long distance movement of people and freight is a sign of modernisation and efficiency. Model 1 is transforming society and economy as profoundly as the industrial revolution or the introduction of settled farming at the end of the Neolithic period. Model 1 does not only generate substantial amounts of long distance traffic that needs more and more airports, roads and ports - it requires the fundamental breakdown of local production and consumption links to feed an insatiable appetite for profit, turnover and spatially-fragmented intensive production. Long distance transport is the life-blood of this new order and demands there be no limits on air transport, new motorways or food miles. Unfortunately, some organic food suppliers are following the same pattern in the form of mass production, marketing and long distance distribution. Eating Oil reveals the lunacy of this approach - the cost of damage to the environment, communities, food security and safety are just too high.

Model 2 is the one not on offer to most people in industrialised countries and is an option that is gradually being removed from those in 'developing' nations. It is the one that the democratic process cannot currently deliver, even though we could meet our needs in a socially, environmentally and economically sustainable way. Rather than spending billions on GM technology we could invest in diverse, sustainable food production and supply systems, like organic, which ensure that local agriculture prospers and food is sourced on the basis of the proximity principle. We could encourage farmers in the UK to grow sustainably produced food for local and regional consumption and bring an end to ever increasing levels of food imports and exports.

All this is possible but it is not yet on the political agenda. European governments, with one or two notable exceptions, are bent on large-scale production, globalisation of supply, specialisation and exploiting cheap labour. Solving food miles problems depends absolutely on political will and a strong sense of what is in the public interest. This report provides a comprehensive analysis of the problems facing us and also the solutions - those serving the public interest would be well advised to take note and.......take action.

Professor John Whitelegg

Stockholm Environment Institute, University of York
Professor of Environmental Studies, John Moores University, Liverpool
Visiting Professor of Transport, Roskilde University, Denmark

Contents

Acronyms and Abbreviations

AOA - Agreement on Agriculture
CAP - Common Agricultural Policy
DEFRA - Department of Environment, Food and Rural Affairs
DETR - Department of the Environment, Transport and the Regions (now DEFRA and DTLR)
ECCP - European Climate Change Programme
EEA - European Environment Agency
EU - European Union
FAO - Food and Agriculture Organisation
FMD - Foot and Mouth Disease
FSC - Food Supply Chain
GATT - General Agreement on Tariffs and Trade
IFOAM - International Federation of Organic Agricultural Movements
IMF - International Monetary Fund
IPCC - Intergovernmental Panel on Climate Change
Kg - Kilogram
Km - Kilometre
KWh - Kilowatt hour
MAFF - Ministry of Agriculture, Fisheries and Food (now DEFRA)
MJ - Megajoule
OPEC - Organisation of Petroleum Exporting Countries
RDC - Regional Distribution Centre
RGV - Road Goods Vehicle
TERN - Trans-European Road Network
UNEP - United Nations Environment Programme
WTO - World Trade Organisation

Summary

Many of the high-profile social, environmental and public health problems within the food system are symptoms of flaws within the farming and food system. One of the most damaging aspects of the contemporary food system is the extent to which the supply of even the most basic foods has become dependent on petroleum.

Fuelling the food system

■ Transporting food long distances is energy inefficient. We put in more energy (in the form of non-renewable fossil fuels) than we get out (in the form of food calories). For every calorie of iceberg lettuce, flown in from Los Angeles, we use 127 calories of fuel.

■ Long distance transport also emits carbon dioxide (CO_2), a greenhouse gas. One sample basket of imported organic produce could release as much CO_2 into the atmosphere as an average four bedroom household does through cooking meals for eight months. The 26 products, collectively, travelled a distance equivalent to six times round the equator (241,000 kilometres).

■ The same basket of non-organic imported produce would do the same damage. However, on top of this, non-organic food uses more energy in the production process.[1] Non-organic milk, for example, needs five times more energy per cow than organic milk.[2]

■ Food packaging also uses energy and creates pollution. Most of the 80 million food and drinks cans we use each day are not recycled but buried, in increasingly scarce landfill sites.[3]

■ International food trade is increasing faster than the world's population and food production. Between 1968 and 1998, world food production increased by 84%, population by 91% and food trade by 184%.[4]

■ UK imports and exports of many food products have increased in recent decades. The situation for certain food categories is now critical. For example, even if all UK fruit production went to UK consumption, out of 100 purchases, on average only 5 will have been grown in the UK.

■ Rather than importing what they cannot produce themselves, many countries appear to be simply 'swapping food'. In 1997, the UK imported 126 million litres of milk and exported 270 million litres.[5]

■ The organic sector seems to be repeating these trends, with UK imports of meat growing from 5% of the market in 1998/9 to 30% in 1999/2000.[6] Of all organic food consumed in the UK, three-quarters is imported. This is because UK farmers, like their conventional counterparts, cannot supply large volumes of standard produce all year round, to the major retailers who dominate the distribution system.

■ One study has estimated that UK imports of food products and animal feed involved transportation by sea, air and road amounting to over 83 billion tonne-kilometres, using 1.6 billion litres of fuel and, resulting in 4.1 million tonnes of carbon dioxide emissions.[7]

■ Some types of food will always have to be imported, but some forms of freight transport are much less environmentally damaging than others. Shipping is one of the best options, since road transport generates six times more CO_2 and airfreight 50 times more.[8]

■ Unfortunately, between 1989 and 1999 there was a 90% increase in road freight movements of agricultural and food products between the UK and Europe.[9] Worse still, total UK airfreight doubled over the same period, and is predicted to increase at 7.5% each year until 2010.[10]

■ Despite aviation causing more environmental damage than road transport, there is no tax on aviation fuel. In November 2000 a motorist paid 80p for a litre of unleaded petrol, and airlines paid 18p for a litre of fuel.[11]

■ Once inside the UK, food continues to clock up food miles. Between 1978 and 1999 we consumed 9% more food, feed and drink, but transported 16% more and over distances that were 50% longer. The food system accounts for up to 40 per cent of all UK road freight.[12]

■ We are driving further to shop, and more frequently, including for our food. Between 1985/6 and 1996/8 average distances increased 57% (from 14 to 22 Kilometres) and frequency from 1.68 to 2.42 times a week.[13]

Why do we have a problem?

■ OPEC Petroleum Exporting Countries, mainly in the Middle East, account for some 40% of world oil production, and almost two-thirds of oil reserves are in the Middle East. The political and economic conditions, which led to the first oil crisis of 1973, remain largely the same.

■ If consumption remains constant, oil reserves could be exhausted by 2040.[14] However, consumption is not constant. In 1985, Asia consumed 18% of the world's oil. By 1997, this increased to 26.4%.[15] Consumption in developed countries continues to be significant.

■ Even if new oil reserves are found, the climate change consequences of using them could be catastrophic. The 1990s was the warmest decade, globally, since instrument records began in 1861. Droughts, floods, rising sea levels and ecological disasters are predicted to increase in frequency and spread. Food security in the world's poorest regions is at particular risk from climate change.[16]

■ The Intergovernmental Panel on Climate change (IPCC), an international group of 2,500 of the world's experts in this area, has recommended cuts of 60-80% of greenhouse gasses just to stabilise the situation.[17]

■ The Kyoto protocol, the international agreement to cut greenhouse gasses, does not include emissions from international sea and airfreight, so there is currently no incentive to reduce them.

■ The food system is a significant contributor to climate change. A typical UK family of four would, each year, emit 4.2 tonnes of CO_2 from their house, 4.4 tonnes from their car, and 8 tonnes from the production, processing, packaging and distribution of the food they eat.

■ As well as climate change, road transport also contributes to ill health (through accidents and air pollution). Government experts reported, in 1998, that between 12,000 and 24,000 people might die prematurely each year from air pollution.[18] Vehicle manufacture and transport infrastructure, such as roads, ports and airports, further contribute to CO_2 emissions and environmental damage.

■ Oil spills from tankers sporadically devastate marine life and sea birds. The world's largest spill - from the Amoco Cadiz in 1978 - oiled 25,000 birds in Brittany.[19]

■ Some studies show that, specialisation and standardisation, coupled with long distance transport is diluting the nutritional potency of our food. Some nutrient losses, in particular vitamin C, vitamin A, riboflavin and vitamin E, will occur even with excellent storage conditions.[20][21]

■ Growing crops for export - through the same process of specialisation and standardisation - is threatening the genetic diversity of plants and animals. More than 700 breeds of farm animals are already extinct. In the Philippines, where thousands of traditional rice varieties were once cultivated by small farmers, just two varieties accounted for 98 per cent of all rice production in the mid-1980s.[22]

■ In 1998, 12.3 million pigs, cattle and sheep were traded, live, within the EU.[23] Despite animal welfare legislation, many animals die on route while others are in a pitiful state when they arrive at their destination, after hours in miserable conditions.

■ Transporting live animals and meat products increases the risk of spreading disease, which threatens livelihoods as well as human and animal health. One estimate of losses due to Food and Mouth disease was put at £9 billion, and some four million animals have been slaughtered.

■ Food trade is said to help poor countries to develop their economies and break out of poverty. However, a recent UN report on the world's 48 poorest countries showed that although they had opened their economies to imports and exports, poverty had deepened.[24] In addition, once a producer grows for export, considerable and growing levels of external inputs are required to compete effectively.

■ Over a period when Kenyan fruit exports almost doubled, domestic consumption declined from 30.5 to 26.5 kilograms of fruit per person per year.[25] In addition, as a result of pressure for fresh produce, 93 per cent of Kenya's fresh horticultural exports to the UK are airfreighted.[26]

■ Competition between horticultural producers in developing countries compounds market uncertainty and means that they are in a similar, vulnerable situation to the producers of more traditional cash crops like coffee.

■ The poor human rights record of many oil producing countries also hinders development. An estimated 10,000 families, from each of the six major oil producing regions in Nigeria, have lost their farmlands to oil production and transport alone.[27]

Creating a more sustainable food supply

■ The current food system is linear in design, treating inputs such as energy and raw materials as infinitely available (which they are not), and the environment as infinitely capable of absorbing waste (which it is not). We need to move away from these unsustainable linear systems towards more sustainable circular approaches.

■ Organic production systems are an example of the sustainable, circular methods of food production, and sales of organic food more than doubled from £260 million in 1997/8 to £605 million in 1999/2000. Unfortunately, the sustainable system is fractured by organic imports, sucked in to fill the gap between domestic demand and supply.

■ The transport involved in importing organic products consumes more energy than is saved through organic production. For instance, when organic produce is imported by plane from New Zealand, the transport energy consumption is 235 times greater than the energy savings of organic production.

■ The loop could be closed by increasing organic production in the UK (via targets for organic production and an action plan to meet them), diversifying production and encouraging consumers to chose more sustainable options which minimise food miles such as farmers markets, box schemes, farm shops and community food growing schemes .

■ The proximity principle suggests that production should be located as close as possible to the consumer. If, for example, locally grown spring onions were brought through a home delivery box scheme, there would be 300 times less CO_2 emissions than if they were flown in from Mexico and brought from a supermarket in a shopping trip by car.

■ Local food systems also generate jobs, as citizens as far apart as Cornwall and Austria are discovering through their own schemes.

■ Some foods will always be supplied from outside the UK, simply because they cannot be produced in temperate climates. Much of this is already transported by ship - the least environmentally damaging option - but still more benefits can be gained through fair trade, where suppliers receive a reasonable and secure income.

Conclusions and recommendations

■ Government currently appears to hold two mutually incompatible positions: first, that it is committed to a sustainable farming and food system, second that it cannot introduce policies to promote such a system due to the constrains of globalisation and the need to be internationally competitive.

■ Of the three complimentary approaches we have identified to help relocalise food systems, one requires no Government action. The farming and food sector could voluntarily opt to steadily increase the proportion of local produce they buy and sell. Imaginative, voluntary labelling schemes could highlight the environmental benefits of buying local.

■ The other two approaches need leadership, and action by government. Environmental taxes, for example, are one way to show the real cost of using oil and its products, which are not currently reflected in the price of petrol and, particularly, aviation fuel.

■ Other fiscal measures, for example, subsidies for local food production may be more politically acceptable than taxes but would need to be set in the context of a comprehensive action plan, with targets, for sustainable food production systems.

The report makes comprehensive recommendations for action by individuals, industry, local and national government and the public interest sector. The primary recommendations are:

1) Developing a sustainable food system should become a major government policy based on setting targets for sustainable food production, import substitution, fair trade and local sourcing of food to be achieved over a specific period.

2) Measures should be introduced to internalise the external environmental and social costs of transportation to minimise the damaging effects of international and national food freight transport by air and road and shopping by car.

3) Agricultural support policies should be redirected specifically to promote sustainable food production and localised food sourcing and processing.

4) Fiscal measures such as tax incentives should be introduced to encourage businesses and public sector bodies to buy food from local or regional suppliers.

5) Labelling on all food products should be introduced to indicate the environmental impact of distribution. Organic and other assurance schemes should take the lead by introducing the proximity principle into certification.

6) More research is urgently required into the obstacles to and benefits from changing to a localised food system.

1) The purpose of this report

"The justification by modernity, rationalism and efficiency to produce food of mediocre nutritive quality, some of which is even dangerous for health, is absolutely scandalous. Does this 'progress' in fact hide a kind of regression? Fear of eating one's steak is equivalent to returning to the stone-age. The debate on food is therefore a fundamental debate on health and lifestyle. On another level, that of quantity, a more global geopolitical debate exists on 'who should feed whom?' and on the types of food production which best respect the environment. Although Europe exports cereals, to produce them it imports oil" Matthieu Calame and Philippe Cacciabue.[28]

Consumer confidence in food has been severely damaged in recent years, the agricultural economy is in turmoil and the Common Agricultural Policy (CAP) is under review. This situation presents an opportunity to develop a sustainable food system. Many commentators have described farming as being at a crossroads. If so, policy-makers and consumers should be aware of the options available and the consequences of purchasing decisions and policies that affect the way in which food is produced, processed, distributed and retailed.

These issues have been addressed in previous reports by the SAFE Alliance and Sustain and by other organisations and institutes.[29] However, recent events in UK farming as a whole, as well as in the organic sector, require further examination. UK imports and exports of foodstuffs have increased in recent decades and there will be a further expansion in international trade in food if policies to promote trade liberalisation are implemented. Research by Sustain in 1999, revealed that there had been no reduction in the distance that food is transported within the UK. Despite claims of local and regional sourcing by the multiple retailers, a recent survey found that very few products sold in supermarkets are supplied directly by local farms.[30]

Although progress has been disappointing, the goal remains to identify and promote sustainable food supply chains which meet nutritional needs, which minimise environmental damage and ensure that producers receive a decent income. To reach this goal we need to assess processing, packaging and distribution as well as food production. In short we must consider food supply chains in their entirety.

We also need to explore alternatives to the predominant production, packaging, distribution and marketing systems or risk overlooking the most sustainable options. For example, at present a large proportion of the organic and non-organic food consumed in the UK is imported, marketed at supermarkets and purchased in shopping trips by car. In this report local and regional food sourcing systems are also evaluated, together with local marketing systems such as farmers' markets and home-delivery box schemes.

The main message of this report is that virtually all of the processes in the modern food system are now dependent upon crude oil, so food supply chains produce large quantities of greenhouse gas emissions. We calculate the transport-related emissions of the main greenhouse gas, carbon dioxide, associated with food distribution in the UK and shopping by car, along with imports of various food products by air, ship and road. If a product can be sourced in the UK, we compare international and local sourcing on the basis of fuel consumption and carbon dioxide emissions.

In undertaking this analysis, it has remained clear that consumers are often unaware of the environmental, social and economic impact of the products that they purchase and are not only physically but also 'psychologically' distanced from the contemporary food system (see **Box 1**).[31] The extent of this 'information gap' has been highlighted in surveys of school children and in the public reaction to the few reports and analyses that have assessed transport in food supply chains.[32] One way to communicate this information to a consumer is an environmental label. This report outlines the options for a transport-related environmental indicator for fresh produce, and for including transport issues in organic standards.

In developing a sustainable food system, the organic sector could be leading the way. The direct environmental and ecological impact of agriculture 'on the farm' is certainly reduced through organic practices. However, little attention has been paid to the transport costs associated with farm inputs and, more importantly, with the distribution of organic products to the consumer. At present the UK imports around three-quarters of its organic food compared to about a third for all food products. This results in significant environmental costs. Additionally, if organic foods that could be produced in the UK continue to be imported in large quantities this could hinder conversion here. As food is travelling ever further within and between countries, it is important that consumers, of organic food products, in particular, are aware of the environmental impact of all transport involved in supplying these items. Alternative marketing systems exist which are, and will continue to be, based on local and regional sourcing and this report concludes with recommendations to encourage these options.

Box 1 Public awareness of the origin and seasonality of food

A survey of 8- to 11-year-olds, commissioned by the National Farmers Union (NFU)[33], found:

■ Nearly half think margarine comes from cows
■ One in five do not know that ham comes from pigs, including one child who was convinced it comes from deer
■ Nearly a third believe oranges are grown in Britain
■ Three quarters do not know that sugar beet - one of the country's biggest crops - is grown in Britain
■ A quarter do not know that peas are grown in Britain
■ Six in ten do not know spinach is grown in Britain

Another national survey revealed that the British public wants to buy home-grown food in season but has lost touch with when it is harvested.[34] The MORI survey found:

■ 74 per cent of people say they would be likely to buy British fruit and vegetables when they are in season
■ 56 per cent of those who would buy seasonal produce say they would do so to support the rural economy
■ other main reasons for buying in season fruit and vegetables are freshness (31 per cent), good taste (23 per cent) and good quality (20 per cent)

But the responses also revealed:

■ 70 per cent of people do not know that home-grown peas are harvested from May to June
■ 54 per cent do not know that British new potatoes are available from May to June

2) The contemporary food system

In industrialised countries such as Britain, food supply is now synonymous with convenience, extensive choice, and the year-round availability of both processed and fresh produce. Food production, distribution and retailing systems have undergone significant change and as a result there are fundamental differences between the contemporary food system and its counterpart 50 or even 30 years ago. There have been a number of drivers that have shaped the contemporary food system. These include:

- the modernisation of agriculture and, in the European Union (EU), the introduction of the Common Agricultural Policy (CAP);
- a shift away from local supply of and demand for primary agricultural produce and towards more international trade, which has resulted in increasingly global food supply chains;
- the provision of transport infrastructure and low transport costs;
- the emergence of the multiple retailers, which increasingly co-ordinate the production, processing and distribution of food products;
- demographic and lifestyle changes, in industrialised countries such as the UK, that have resulted in a polarisation of consumers - a small but growing proportion demanding healthy, ethically-produced organic food, while the majority focus on price and convenience; and
- IMF and World Bank policies that have encouraged food production for export and the opening up of domestic markets to food imports in less industrialised, poorer countries.

At the same time, the food system has never had such a high profile or been the focus of so many concerns. These are diverse and include: a series of food safety issues; concerns about national food security and the rural economy due to increased food imports; the health implications of poor diets; the ecological consequences of intensive agricultural production; animal welfare standards and the demise of small mixed farms and independent grocers. The way in which food is produced, distributed and marketed has increasingly been a focus of attention for consumers, environmental groups, policy-makers and the food producers – the farmers and horticulturists – themselves.[35] There is a growing recognition that there are significant adverse environmental, social and economic effects associated with food production, packaging, distribution and marketing systems. Food is a basic human need and food supply is therefore a good place to start when identifying sustainable options for meeting our needs. The first step in the process of developing a more sustainable food system is gaining a deeper understanding of the present situation.[36]

A farming crisis...

Farming in the UK is experiencing perhaps its worst ever crisis. The average UK farmer earned just £5,200 for the financial year to February 2001. The total income from farming for 2000 fell 27 per cent in real terms to £1.88 billion, down by more than two-thirds in the five years from 1996, when it was more than £5 billion.[37] Agricultural borrowing continues to rise and stands at an estimated all-time high of more than £10 billion, while investment is at its lowest level since the 1970s. In the two years to June 2000, 51,300 farmers and farm workers lost their livelihoods in agriculture.[38] However, towards the other end of the food chain the multiple retailers continue to make substantial annual profits and to benefit from the changes in food production and trade in recent decades. In the UK the five largest retail chains account for 80 per cent of the market[39], and their marketing decisions have a massive effect on producers, other retailers and the environment. The supermarkets exert a virtual monopoly over many towns and villages, so many consumers have little choice but to shop at the major multiples.[40] A recent survey found that 94 per cent of those interviewed who had responsibility for food shopping bought most of their food at supermarkets.[41] In April 2001 Tesco became the second UK retailer to join the billion-pound profits club, and now aims to recreate its domestic success overseas by opening chains across the globe from Poland to South Korea.[42]

The recent Foot and Mouth Disease (FMD) outbreak is not an isolated incident in the recent history of farming in the UK. Food production and distribution in the UK has been connected to a series of food safety issues and outbreaks of animal diseases (see **Section 4.8**). These have included salmonella in poultry and eggs in the 1980s, BSE in cattle in the 1990s, and swine fever which hit the pig industry in Essex in August 2000.

These events are symptoms of the problems within farming and the food system. Farmers have to minimise production costs and maximise yields in order to compete internationally with crop and livestock operations outside the UK. These are often large-scale and based on industrial techniques requiring high levels of inputs such as feed, pesticides, fertilisers and machinery. As the external environmental and social costs associated with the production, supply and use of these inputs are not accounted for, economies of scale are rewarded as production costs are artificially low. International sourcing by retailers and processors is resulting in ever-increasing levels of international trade in food and centralised distribution in the UK means that UK food products and imports are transported long distances by lorry due to a concentration in food processing and retailing (**Section 3.4**).

Despite the farming crisis, over forty per cent of the total EU budget is still spent on the Common Agricultural Policy. However, of this, 80 per cent goes to 20 per cent of the wealthiest farmers while the rest struggle. In 1999 the EU was paying an average subsidy of £11,790 per farmer, which cost the average British family £10 per week. The Common Agricultural Policy (CAP) stands accused of overseeing a system of European agriculture that causes enormous damage to the environment and rural livelihoods.[43] It has encouraged larger, more intensive farms at the expense of smaller, more sustainable ones, leads to inhumane treatment of animals through live exports, and generates apparently cheap food at enormous hidden expense to all of us – through the health budget, the environmental clean-up budget, and compensation to farmers for livestock diseases such as BSE and Foot and Mouth Disease (FMD).[44]

Indeed, it has been estimated that the total hidden or 'external' social and environmental costs of non-organic farming in the UK alone amounts to £2.34 billion per year (based on 1996 data), or £208 per hectare.[45] This is in addition to the costs of the CAP subsidy which supports EU farmers to the tune of over £30 billion each year. Organic farming, by contrast, with only one third of the hidden costs of non-organic agriculture, has the potential to reduce the external costs of UK agriculture by £1.6 billion, or £120 - £140 per hectare.[46]

...and a fuel and food crisis

However, arguably the most damaging, dangerous and certainly the least noticed aspect of the contemporary food system is the extent to which the supply of even the most basic foods has become dependent on petroleum. We caught a glimpse of this dependence in the UK in September 2000, when blockades at oil refineries and distribution depots by protestors, consisting mainly of farmers and road hauliers, resulted in a national 'fuel crisis'. Within days the supermarkets began to ration sales of bread, milk and sugar. The chief executive of Sainsbury's, one of the largest retailers in the UK, wrote to the Prime Minister to warn that the petrol crisis was threatening Britain's food stocks and that stores were likely to be out of food in "days rather than weeks."[47] Ironically, one of the main aims of post-war UK agricultural policy has been to avoid food shortages and ensure food security, which were also the original goals of the CAP. Food security is now seriously under threat due to the dependency of the food system on fuels derived from crude oil and the very real possibility of disruptions in oil supplies, which would quickly result in food shortages (see **Section 4.1**).

Sudden changes such as: a conflict in oil producing regions; increases in oil prices; strikes and blockades; or a poor harvest in the country of origin, could in a short timescale, lead to food supplies being disrupted. The price of oil, for example, has fluctuated significantly in recent decades and is likely to continue to do so in the near future. It is evident in the case of imports, that days before the food product is available to the consumer, the product could be thousands of kilometres away. The fuel crisis also demonstrated the vulnerability of the 'just-in-time' supply policy of multiple retailers, in which even UK-supplied foodstuffs are hundreds of kilometres away from the store the day before they are due to be delivered. The use of regional distribution centres and refrigerated transportation is therefore not only transport intensive and polluting but also highly dependent on petroleum. If oil prices increase sharply then increases in food prices are likely follow and when oil or petroleum supplies are disrupted there will be empty shelves at supermarkets.

Climate change, which a majority in the scientific community now accept is taking place, will also threaten food security. In order to reduce concentrations of greenhouse gases in the atmosphere the Intergovernmental Panel on Climate Change (IPCC), has recommended cuts of 60-80 per cent in greenhouse gas emissions. This report will try to identify the food supply chains which contribute most to this reduction.

The pound in whose pocket?

Fifty years ago, at least half of each pound spent on food found its way back to the farmer and rural community.[48] The rest was spread amongst suppliers of agricultural inputs and manufacturers, processors and retailers. However, in recent decades the balance of power has shifted away from the 'middle ground', with value captured on the input side by agrochemical, feed and seed companies, and on the output side by those who distribute, process and sell food.[49] This is a significant development which helps to explain the decline in farming and rural areas worldwide. As farmers now get a much smaller share, no more than 10-20 per cent, and they also pass on less, spending less in rural communities, employing fewer local people.[50] It also demonstrates that the move away from a food system based largely on a local and regional level to one that is global, inevitably means that there are more stages between farm and consumer, and each eats into farmers' profits. This is compounded by trends towards processed food products and the dominance of multiple retailers, whose buying power allows them to source food from where it can be produced at the lowest cost, forcing farmers everywhere to compete with overseas producers.

In the UK, the increase in the market share of the multiple retailers has been accompanied by a decline in local retailers and the independent grocery sector in particular. A report by the National Retail Planning Forum has identified the loss of 25,000 jobs (mostly in small shops) within a ten mile radius of 93 superstores over a three year period – an average of 270 in each location.[51] More than 80 per cent of grocery sales are now at supermarkets with much less benefit to the local economy and local community.[52]

Rapid globalisation and low transportation costs have resulted in increased agricultural specialisation and production for export. As a result, farmers are vulnerable to economic vagaries throughout the world, and events like the 1998 Asian economic downturn can directly affect UK farm income. Furthermore, the UK now imports a variety of foods that were once grown here. All this is possible because prices and policies do not recognise the social and environmental costs of transportation such as greenhouse gas emissions.[53] Given the threat to fuel supplies it is clear that policies must now be introduced to develop a sustainable food system. This report details these costs and sets out the options for a more secure food system and the steps we need to take to get there.

3) Fuelling the food system - How dependent is our food supply on non-renewable energy?

Eating Oil was the title of a book published in 1978 following the first oil crisis in 1973.[54] The aim was to investigate the extent to which food supply in industrialised countries relied on fossil fuels, given concerns about oil supplies from the Middle East. In the summer of 2000 degree of dependence on oil in the UK food system was demonstrated once again when protestors blockaded oil refineries and fuel distribution depots. The 'fuel crisis' disrupted the distribution of food and industry leaders warned that their stores would be out of food within days. The oil crisis in 1973 should have been taken as a warning. Food supply should not be so dependent on one finite energy source that cannot be produced in most countries.

However, if anything has changed since the 1970s it is that the food system is now even more dependent on cheap crude oil. Every time we eat, we are all essentially 'eating oil'.

3.1 Households eating oil

One indicator of the unsustainability of the contemporary food system is the ratio of energy outputs - the energy content of a food product (more commonly known as calories) - to the energy inputs. The latter is sometimes referred to as the embodied energy of a food product and is all energy consumed in producing, processing, packaging and distributing that product. The energy ratio (energy out/energy in) in agriculture has decreased from being close to 100 for traditional pre-industrial societies to less than 1 in most cases in the present food system, as energy inputs, mainly in the form of fossil-fuels, have gradually increased.

In modern high input fruit and vegetable cultivation, the output/input ratio is between 2 and 0.1 (i.e. 1 calorie of food energy output requires between 0.5 and 10 calories of energy input, respectively). For intensive beef production the ratio is between 0.1 and 0.03, and may reach extreme values of 0.002 for winter greenhouse vegetables.[55] All of these ratios refer only to the energy consumed up to the farm gate and exclude processing, packaging and distribution.

However, this report shows that transport energy consumption can also be significant, and if included in these ratios would mean that the ratio of food energy to embodied energy would decrease further. A kilogram of apples typically contains 2.31 MJ of nutritional energy. One study has shown that the ratio of the calorific energy content (output) to transport energy (input) for apples ranges from infinity (true environmental sustainability) in the cases where there is no transportation (home grown and locally sourced apples) to a minimum ratio value of 0.13 when the product is imported (by ship), distributed centrally and purchased at a supermarket in a shopping trip by car.[56] The ratio is even more staggering when food is airlifted. For example, when iceberg lettuce is imported to the UK from the USA by plane, the energy ratio, in this instance the ratio of the calorific content - to the energy inputs - the energy consumed in this single transport step, is 0.00786. In other words 127 calories of energy (aviation fuel) are needed to transport 1 calorie of lettuce across the Atlantic. If the energy consumed during lettuce cultivation, packaging, refrigeration, distribution in the UK and shopping by car was included the energy needed would be even higher. Similarly, 97 calories of transport energy are needed to import 1 calorie of asparagus by plane from Chile, and 66 units of energy are consumed when flying 1 unit of carrot energy from South Africa.

This reliance on an energy source that is consumed more quickly than it can be regenerated is obviously not sustainable. The present system can only exist as long as inexpensive fossil fuels are available (see Section 4.1).[57]

Table 1 shows the energy consumption and carbon dioxide emissions when importing foodstuffs, in this case, organic food products to the UK by plane.[58] The carbon dioxide emissions range from 1.6 kilograms to 10.7 kilograms. A comparison with domestic appliances shows the magnitude of the environmental effects. For example, in terms of energy consumption, importing a kilogram of spinach, strawberries or lettuce from California is equivalent to operating a 100 watt light bulb continuously for 8 days. Similarly, a kilogram of food imported almost 19,000 kilometres by plane from New Zealand results in the same quantity of carbon dioxide emitted when boiling a kettle 268 times.

Table 1 The carbon dioxide emissions, energy and fuel consumption when importing various organic products by plane[59]

Product	Origin	Distance (kilometres)	CO2 Emissions (grammes)	Energy Consumption (MJ)	Fuel Consumption (litres)
			Per kilogram of food		
Strawberries, Cherries, Peppers, Herbs	Ankara, Turkey	2835	1616.0	24.24	0.64
Strawberries, Green Beans, Salad Onions, Garden Peas, Sugar Snaps,	Cairo, Egypt	3520	2006.4	30.10	0.80
Fine Beans, Mangetout, Sugar Snaps, Courgettes, Salad Onions,	Nairobi, Kenya	6804	3878.3	58.17	1.54
Chanterelle Mushrooms, various vegetables,	Lusaka, Zambia	7905	4505.9	67.59	1.79
Herbs	Harare, Zimbabwe	8257	4706.5	70.60	1.87
Strawberries, Baby Spinach, Raspberries, Watercress, Rocket, Lettuce, Limes, Peeled Baby Carrots, Cherry Tomatoes, Herbs, Garlic, Cranberries, Cherries, Broccoli, Green Beans	Los Angeles, California	8774	5001.2	75.02	1.98
Broccoli	Guatemala City, Guatemala	8782	5005.7	75.09	1.99
Avocados, Cherry Tomatoes, Mangoes, Limes,	Mexico City, Mexico	8941	5096.4	76.44	2.02
Ginger,	Rio de Janeiro, Brazil	9307	5305.0	79.57	2.11
Mangetout, Fine Beans, Runner Beans, Herbs, Asparagus,	Bangkok, Thailand	9534	5434.4	81.52	2.16
Avocados, Baby Carrots, Asparagus, Radish, Peppers, Grapes,	Cape Town, South Africa	9622	5484.5	82.27	2.18
Garlic,	Buenos Aires, Argentina	11082	6316.7	94.75	2.51
Raspberries, Kiwi Fruit, Asparagus, Grapes, Plums, Blackberries,	Valparaiso, Chile	11663	6647.9	99.72	2.64
Beef Cuts, Ginger	Melbourne, Australia	16913	9640.4	144.60	3.83
Blueberries	Wellington, New Zealand	18839	10738.2	161.07	4.26

Figure 1 provides examples of carbon dioxide emissions from transporting organic food imports. In this instance, transporting these 26 organic items from source to the home results in 84 kg of carbon dioxide emissions. This is only slightly less than 1 per cent of annual UK per capita carbon dioxide emissions. Moving of these imported products from point of departure to point of entry in the UK accounts for the majority of the emissions (82 kilograms CO2) and taking them from the store to the home in a shopping trip by car adds 1.8 kilograms of carbon dioxide emissions. This is equivalent, in climate change terms, to releasing the same amount of carbon dioxide into the atmosphere as an average four-bedroom household does through cooking in eight months.

The transport-related carbon dioxide emissions associated with this single shopping basket are equivalent to 8 per cent of the average annual per capita carbon dioxide emissions in Africa. If a shopping basket of this type was purchased each week, the associated carbon dioxide emissions each year would be greater than world average per capita emissions of 4 tonnes per year.

The transport-related environmental effects would be exactly the same for non-organic foods imported from each of the countries listed in **Figure 1** and **Table 1**. However, non-organic produce would cause more environmental damage due to the use of synthetic fertilisers and pesticides during production. Although organic production is more environmentally efficient, the benefit of this can be offset by long distance distribution.

In 1999 the average per capita carbon dioxide emissions in the UK was 9.63 tonnes per person per year. This figure is obtained in a simple calculation in which all UK fossil fuel related carbon dioxide emissions, resulting from transportation, industry, household activities and other sources are divided by the number of UK inhabitants. However, the carbon dioxide emissions resulting from the international transportation associated with imports are not included in annual per capita emissions. If they were, then UK per capital greenhouse gas emissions would be significantly greater. Assuming that the food items in **Figure 1** are for a family of four and that similar carbon dioxide emissions result from grocery purchases each week, then this would add 1.1 tonnes of carbon dioxide to annual per capita emissions. Current estimates of carbon dioxide emissions are therefore unrealistic and provide no incentive to reduce the emissions associated with food imports.

Clearly, if other imported household and commercial items, as well as food, were included in the UK inventory, per capita carbon dioxide emissions would be considerably greater than the current figure of around 10 tonnes per capita per year.

Figure 1 The transport-related carbon dioxide emissions associated with a basket of imported organic food products[60]

MULTIPLE PROBLEMS

TEL 920 1853 7415

Hidden Costs - What a bargain!
These are some of the costs not included in the price of these imported organic products

	CO2 (grammes)	Distance (kilometres)
DUTCH CUCUMBER 0.5 kg	10	100
DANISH BUTTER 0.5 kg	24	1189
ITALIAN LEMONS 0.4 kg	43	1738
SPANISH PEPPERS 0.6kg	58	1542
SPANISH CELERY 0.6 kg	58	1542
SPANISH AUBERGINE 1.2 kg	131	1542
AUSTRALIAN BEEF JOINT 1.6 kg	343	21466
NEW ZEALAND ONIONS 1.8 kg	414	22992
WASHINGTON STATE APPLES 3 kg	489	16307
SICILIAN POTATOES 5 kg	771	2448
3 BOTTLES NEW ZEALAND WINE 3.6 kg	828	22992
ARGENTINIAN GARLIC 0.2 kg	1263	11082
TANZANIAN HONEY 0.5 kg	2114	7419
ZAMBIAN MUSHROOMS 0.5 kg	2253	7905
KENYAN SALAD ONIONS 0.6 kg	2327	6804
CALIFORNIAN BABY SPINACH 0.6 kg	3001	8774
CALIFORNIAN CHERRIES 0.6 kg	3001	8774
GUATEMALAN BROCCOLI 0.9 kg	4505	8782
CALIFORNIAN STRAWBERRIES 1 kg	5001	8774
THAI RUNNER BEANS 1 kg	5434	9534
MEXICAN AVOCADOS 1.1 kg	5606	8941
CHILEAN ASPARAGUS 1 kg	6648	11663
CHILEAN GRAPES 1 kg	6648	11663
MEXICAN CHERRY TOMATOES 1.8 kg	9173	8941
NEW ZEALAND BLUEBERRIES 1 kg	10738	18839
SOUTH AFRICAN BABY CARROTS 2 kg	10969	9622
SUBTOTAL	81,853	241,375
Shopping trip of 8.3 km in an average car	1,826	8.3
TOTAL	**83,679**	**241,383**

SIGN UP FOR YOUR GLOBAL WARMING CLUBCARD!
Transporting these products to you has made a significant contribution to climate change by releasing the same amount of carbon dioxide into the atmosphere as an average four-bedroom household does through cooking in eight months.

Key:

imported by plane;   imported by ship;   imported by lorry;

Although it is difficult to say how far, on average, the food purchased in a shopping trip has travelled, a distance of 3,000 kilometres for a typical supermarket trolley of food is often quoted.[61] The total distance will depend on the number of items purchased, the season, the fraction imported, and the distance between country of origin and the UK. However, it is likely that for many shopping trips, the food purchased will have travelled considerably further than 3,000 kilometres. For example, if a single food product is imported by plane from Egypt, California or New Zealand the distances involved are 3500, 8700 and 18800 kilometres, respectively. If a shopping basket contains foodstuffs from all three of these countries the cumulative distance will be at least 31,000 kilometres. In **Figure 1** the total distance involved in transporting the 26 imported food products is over 241,000km. The equatorial circumference of the Earth is 40,075 kilometres, which means that the cumulative distance these products have travelled is equivalent to being transported around the globe six times.

The example below demonstrates the distances accumulated and the resulting carbon dioxide emissions when the ingredients for a 'traditional' Sunday meal are imported. If these foods were purchased in a shopping trip the trolley would, in effect, have travelled over 49 thousand miles or 81 thousand kilometres (**Table 2**). This is equivalent to two journeys around the earth. In terms of greenhouse gas emissions, the single transport stage between point of departure and entry into the UK results in over 37 kilograms of carbon dioxide emissions. This is equivalent to the carbon dioxide emissions when leaving on a 100 watt light bulb continuously for 36 days or 14 weeks worth of cooking in an average four-person household. If these food products were produced and consumed within a 30 mile radius, the transport-related carbon dioxide emissions would be only 58.2 grammes.

Local sourcing through a farmers market, for example, would therefore reduce the greenhouse gas emissions associated with distribution by a factor of 650, i.e. to 0.2 per cent.

In the UK, buying most of these fresh products locally would be possible only during the summer due to seasonal availability. However, different vegetables are available in the UK through the year and the fruits and vegetables shown in **Table 2** could either be stored or preserved to extend their availability.

Table 2 The carbon dioxide emissions when supplying the ingredients for a 'traditional' Sunday meal[62]

Product	Origin	Distance (Miles)	Mode of Transport	Quantity (kilograms)	Carbon Dioxide Emissions (g)
Beef Joint	Australia	13339	ship	1.6	343
Potatoes	Italy	1521	truck	5	771
Carrots	South Africa	5979	plane	2	10969
Broccoli	Guatemala	5457	plane	0.9	4505
Runner Beans	Thailand	5924	plane	1	5434
Total (a)		32220			22022
Blueberries	New Zealand	11706	plane	1	10738
Strawberries	California	5452	plane	1	5001
Total (b)		17158			15739
Grand Total (a+b)		49378			37761

3.2 Producing the food

Massive infusions of energy are now required to manufacture and supply farm machinery, fertilisers, pesticides and feed.[63] There has been an increase in the use of these inputs in recent decades, for example, trade in pesticides and fertiliser use increased by 160 per cent and 18 per cent, respectively, between 1980 and 1998.[64] The manufacture of nitrogen fertilisers is particularly energy intensive which itself has implications for greenhouse gas emissions.

Energy in organic versus non-organic systems

One of the benefits of organic production is that energy consumption, and therefore fossil fuel consumption and greenhouse gas emissions, is less than that in conventional systems. The energy used in food production is often separated into direct and indirect inputs. Indirect inputs include the manufacture and supply of pesticides, feedstuffs and fertilisers while direct energy inputs are those on the farm, such as machinery. One measure of the energy efficiency of food production that allows a comparison between different farming practices is the energy consumed per unit output, often expressed as the energy consumed per tonne of food produced (MJ/tonne) or the energy consumed per kilogram of food (MJ/kg).

Several factors can influence energy consumption during food production including the size of the holding, the field size, the degree of mechanisation and crop management which includes tillage intensity, manure use and weed control. The use of machinery is often the most significant direct energy input and in organic systems is often replaced by human labour, particularly on smaller holdings.

Any studies that make a direct comparison between organic and conventional systems should take into account any differences in weather, soil and topographical conditions, which can affect yields. As a result, comparisons within a specific region or area of a country are far more likely to be reliable than those between countries.

One study has compared organic and conventional livestock, dairy, vegetable and arable systems in the UK.[65] The results for arable and vegetable production are shown in **Figure 2**. Based on average yields, the energy saving through organic production ranges from 0.14 MJ/kg to 1.79 MJ/kg, with the average for the eight crops considered being 0.68 MJ/kg or 42 per cent.

The improved energy efficiency in organic systems is largely due to lower (or zero) fertiliser and pesticide inputs, which account for half of the energy input in conventional potato and winter wheat production and up to 80 per cent of the energy consumed in some vegetable crops.

In another study carried out across several European countries it was also found that synthetic fertiliser accounted for a large percentage of energy inputs. In the case of wheat cultivation, fertilisers amounted to 51 per cent and pesticides 6 per cent of the total energy consumption.[66]

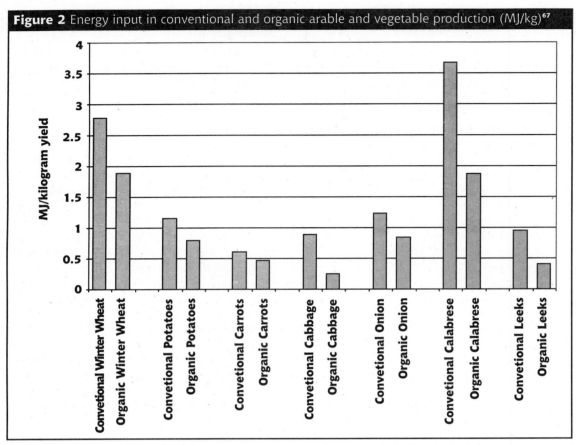

Figure 2 Energy input in conventional and organic arable and vegetable production (MJ/kg)[67]

In conventional upland livestock production, the largest energy input is again indirect in the form of concentrated and cereal feeds. When reared organically, a greater proportion of the feed for dairy cattle, suckler beef and hill sheep is derived from grass. The energy saving through the application of organic livestock practices is even more pronounced than in crop production, with the energy consumption per animal shown in **Figure 3**. In the case of milk production it has been found that organic systems are almost five times more energy efficient on a per animal basis and three and a half times more energy efficient in terms of unit output (the energy required to produce a litre of milk). [68]

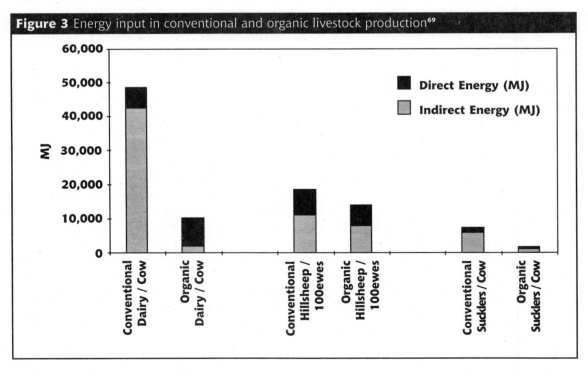

Figure 3 Energy input in conventional and organic livestock production[69]

Similar energy savings have been observed in other countries. For example, a review of cereal production found that low input and organic farms are considerably more energy efficient than high-input systems. For instance high input US maize cultivation uses 4MJ/KG of crop compared to 1.49 MJ in low input systems.[70] For permanent crops, a comparison of conventional and organic olive and citrus farms in Sicily found that organic production results in energy savings of 33 per cent and 45 per cent, respectively.[71]

3.3 Packaging and processing the food

Packaging food is energy intensive and polluting (**Box 2**). In the UK, we produce around 26 million tonnes of household material classified as waste every year, with enough generated each hour to fill the Albert Hall.[72] The majority of this goes to landfill and we fill about 300 million square metres of land with rubbish every year.[73] Household waste is of particular concern because it is made up of many different types of material, which causes problems if not separated in the home for recycling or composting. Domestic waste contains large quantities of organic waste (74 kilograms per person each year) such as food waste, paper and card that can cause pollution problems, including the formation of methane - a powerful greenhouse gas - when in landfill. Plastic packaging is also a problem as recycling has proved difficult and there are now calls for increased incineration of waste as an alternative to landfill. However, burning some plastics produces extremely harmful compounds such as dioxins. These can accumulate in the food chain and affect human health, and have been linked to cancer, reproductive problems and learning difficulties in children. Moreover, incinerators require a steady stream of waste which means that they essentially encourage waste production, rather than reduction, re-use and recycling.[74]

Apart from animal, human and crop waste, the two main types of solid waste generated in the food system are packaging and uneaten food. The average UK family produces three kilograms of packaging waste each week and of the 10-12 kilograms of household food purchases per person per week, on average each household throws away about three kilograms of food.[75] Each year in Britain we throw £500 million of perfectly safe and edible food into landfill sites.[76]

Certain food distribution chains require several types of packaging including:

- primary packaging which contains the food product;
- secondary packaging, such as cases or boxes to carry food products during distribution and for display in shops;
- transit packaging including pallets and plastic wrapping, used to transport, load and unload foodstuffs; and
- boxes or carrier bags which are used to move food products from retail outlets to the home.

The equivalent of 1.5 billion dustbins of packaging waste is produced in the UK each year, most of which ends up in landfill sites.[77] The 3.2 million tonnes of household packaging waste generated each year includes.[78][79]

- 12 billion plastic carrier bags every year, with an average in England of 323 per household. Tesco and Sainsbury alone each hand out one billion. This is enough to cover the whole of London with a layer of bags;
- 15 million plastic bottles every day, of which less than three per cent get recycled;
- Over six billion glass bottles and jars each year; and
- 80 million food and drinks cans every day - one and a half cans per person - which end up being buried in landfill.

Despite the potential to recycle or compost around 70% of household waste, the current recycling rate for the UK is only around 9%, with 82% being buried in landfill sites and 9% incinerated.[80] Disposal to landfill involves high levels of transportation as landfill sites are an increasing distance away from large urban areas where most household waste is generated. We are also rapidly running out of landfill space, with landfill sites in the South East likely to be exhausted by 2004 unless quantities of waste are dramatically reduced.[81]

World-wide production of plastic materials has increased from less than five million tonnes in the 1950s to about 80 million tonnes in 1997. About a third of the total is used in Western Europe with the UK's consumption being just over 3.5 million tonnes. Of all plastics used in the UK each year over 70 per cent (2.5 million tonnes) becomes waste. Approximately 1.5 million tonnes or 60 per cent of all plastic waste is in the form of packaging, and of this half a million tonnes is commercial (distribution and industry) waste and one million tonnes is domestic waste, mainly in the form of food and drinks packaging.[82]

Box 2 Packaging and pollution

a) Asking questions about tomato ketchup can result in red faces

In 1996 researchers at the Swedish Institute for Food and Biotechnology presented the results of an analysis of tomato ketchup.[83] The study considered the production of inputs to agriculture, tomato cultivation and conversion to tomato paste (in Italy), the processing and packaging of the paste and other ingredients into tomato ketchup in Sweden and the retail and storage of the final product. All this involved more than 52 transport and process stages.

The aseptic bags used to package the tomato paste were produced in the Netherlands and transported to Italy to be filled, placed in steel barrels, then moved to Sweden. The five layered, red bottles were either produced in the UK or Sweden with materials form Japan, Italy, Belgium, the USA and Denmark. The polypropylene (PP) screw-cap of the bottle and plug, made from low density polyethylene (LDPE), were produced in Denmark and transported to Sweden. Additionally, LDPE shrink-film and corrugated cardboard, were used to distribute the final product. Labels, glue and ink were not included in the analysis.

This example demonstrates the extent to which the food system is now dependent on national and international freight transport. However, there are many other steps involved in the production of this everyday product. These include the transportation associated with: the production and supply of nitrogen, phosphorus and potassium fertilisers; pesticides; processing equipment and farm machinery. It is possible that other ingredients such as sugar, vinegar, spices and salt are also imported. Most of the processes listed above will also depend on derivatives of fossil fuels such as crude oil, gas and coal. Apart from the fuel used on the farm and during the production and distribution process, crude oil is also required to produce plastics. This product is also likely to be purchased in a shopping trip by car (see **Box 3** and **Section 3.4.6**).

b) Polluting peas?

Another study has compared the energy used in different packaging and sourcing options for garden peas.[84] The results, presented in terms of the energy consumption when producing, packaging and distributing a kilogram of peas, demonstrate the environmental benefits of sourcing food locally when fresh and in season (**Figure 4**). The energy consumed when the peas are processed and packaged ranges from 16-40 MJ/kilogram and is 25 MJ/kilogram for fresh imported peas. However, sourcing fresh peas locally requires only 9 MJ/kilogram, up to 4.4 times less energy than when packaged and processed.

Figure 4 The energy consumed when producing, packaging and distributing a kilogram of peas[85]

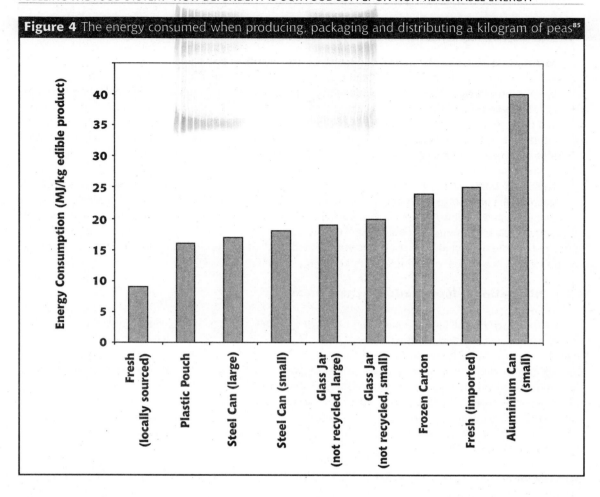

3.4 Distributing the food

The heart of the modern food system is a long, complex distribution system, as these studies reveal:

- The six transport stages involved in distributing imported apples to the household of the UK consumer can use as much as 36-times more energy than commercial apple cultivation.[86]
- One survey looked at organic food imported by multiple retailers that could have been sourced locally.[87] It found green beans are transported 3500 kilometres from Egypt; potatoes 2000 kilometres from Italy; spring onions 9000 kilometres from Mexico; and onions 23,000 kilometres from New Zealand.
- Onions imported from New Zealand will have travelled almost as far as the average UK family car does in the course of a year.[88]
- The energy consumed when carrots are imported from Italy to Sweden could be halved if substituted by carrots grown in Sweden.[89]
- Transporting 1kg of organic blueberries from New Zealand to the UK by plane requires four litres of fuel and results in 10.7 kilograms of carbon dioxide emissions (**Table 1**).

There has been a steady increase in the energy consumption of the transport sector in the UK in recent decades. Transport now accounts for a large proportion of UK energy use and petroleum consumption and, based on government figures, this is predicted to increase. In the UK, transport systems accounted for 54 per cent of petroleum use in 1989 and 62 per cent in 1999.[90] Transportation accounted for 28 per cent of total energy use in the UK in 1986 which increased to 34 per cent in 1999, and in 2020 this sector is predicted to account for 42 per cent of all energy use.[91][92] The Department for the Environment, Transport and the Regions (DETR) has stated that "*Road transport is one of the fastest growing sources of CO2 and accounts for around a fifth of total emissions. Unless action is taken over the next two decades, car traffic could grow by more than a third and van and lorry traffic is forecast to grow even faster. Tackling this growth and reducing transport's impact on the environment is therefore one of the Government's main priorities"* [93]

However, although the transport involved in international trade has been estimated to account for one eighth of world oil consumption[94], and global food production and trade is thought to consume more fossil fuel than any other industrial sector,[401] very few governments have considered import substitution as a means to reduce global greenhouse gas emissions, through reduced international air, sea and road freight transport.

When imports constitute a significant fraction of domestic consumption (as in the case of food in the UK), traditional measures of national energy consumption and emissions become inadequate as indicators of environmental performance. This is because the environmental impact of trade related transportation by sea and air of the product to the UK are not accounted for. Additionally, the environmental damage associated with food production, in the country exporting the product to the UK, will not be allocated to the UK. National figures could show a decline in the fossil fuel energy consumption and air emissions, as well as other indicators relating to the food system such as pesticide use and nitrate levels in water supplies, simply by increasing imports. In reality the environmental impact of food supply could be increasing due to increased international food transportation.

3.4.1 International food trade on the increase

In 1998, over a tenth of all food produced was exported with almost half a billion tonnes more food traded than in 1968. Between 1968 and 1998 world population increased by 91 per cent and there was an 84 per cent increase in world food production (**Table 3**). However, over the same period there was a move to food production for export, which has resulted in even larger increases in international flows of food products. International trade in food almost trebled over this 30-year period, with trade flows doubling for almost every food category (**Figure 5**). In the case of cereals, root crops, vegetable oils, vegetables, fruit, meat and milk, trade increases were at least double those in world production levels. In the case of tree nuts, 39 per cent of world production is exported and for animal fats such as butter and cream, seafood and vegetable oils the corresponding figures are 23 per cent 35 per cent and 43 per cent, respectively.

Increases in global food trade have been facilitated by declining costs of international freight distribution. Sea freight unit costs have fallen by over 70 per cent during the past 20 years, while air freight costs have fallen 3-4 per cent every year.[95]

Table 3 World food production and trade, 1968-1998 [96]

	Production			International Trade		
	Million Metric Tonnes		Change	Million Metric Tonnes		Change
	1968	1998		1968	1998	
Sugar crops	744.7	1510.8	102.9%	0.2	0.1	-50.0%
Animal Fats	21.9	30.8	40.6%	4.5	7.2	60.0%
Seafood	59.9	120.6	101.3%	23.3	42.6	82.8%
Stimulants*	6.5	13	100.0%	5.6	12	114.3%
Sweeteners	80.1	164	104.7%	20.5	45.9	123.9%
Treenuts	3.3	6.7	103.0%	1.1	2.6	136.4%
Eggs	18.6	51.9	179.0%	0.5	1.2	140.0%
Cereals	1064.6	1883.7	76.9%	106.3	271.7	155.6%
Milk	389.5	557	43.0%	25.4	69.2	172.4%
Oil Crops	149.2	453.4	203.9%	20.1	59.9	198.0%
Spices	1.9	4.6	142.1%	0.3	1	233.3%
Starchy Roots	537	647.3	20.5%	8.7	30.5	250.6%
Fruit	223.8	430.9	92.5%	21.8	81.3	272.9%
Meat	94.8	222.4	134.6%	5.6	23	310.7%
Vegetables	251.1	625.1	148.9%	8.7	38.1	337.9%
Offals	7.7	14.9	93.5%	0.3	1.9	533.3%
Vegetable Oils	25	86.2	244.8%	5.1	36.8	621.6%
Pulses	42	56	33.3%	0.2	7.7	3750.0%
Total	3721.6	6879.3	84.8%	258.2	732.7	183.8%

Notes: Figures for international trade are based on data for exports
* tea and coffee

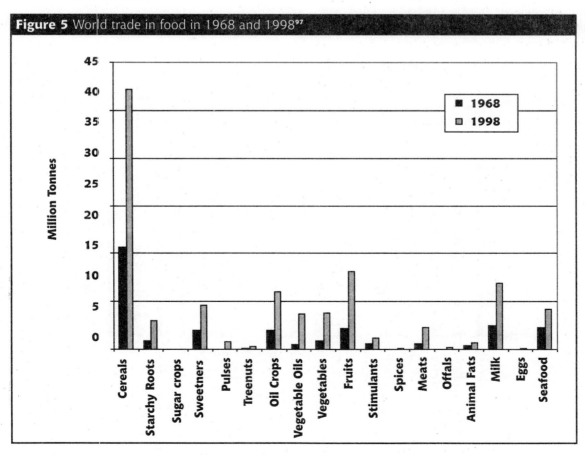

Figure 5 World trade in food in 1968 and 1998[97]

In the UK, between 1968 and 1998 the population increased by 6 per cent and UK food production increased by 34 per cent from 51 million tonnes to over 68.5 million tonnes. The majority of this increased production was exported as UK self-sufficiency in food remained at approximately two-thirds over this period. Although imports increased by over 5 per cent in the three decades up to 1998, food exports increased by 461 per cent and total UK trade in food increased by 50 per cent, from 28 to 41 million tonnes.

Figure 6 shows the products for which there were significant increases in UK imports between 1961 and 1998. During this period fruit imports more than doubled and imports of vegetable oils, starchy roots and vegetables trebled. The situation for certain food categories is now critical (**Figure 7**). For example, of 1000 fruit products purchased in the UK, on average only 6 will have been grown in the UK.

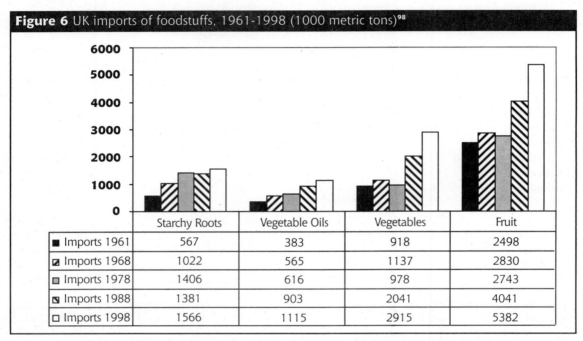

Figure 6 UK imports of foodstuffs, 1961-1998 (1000 metric tons)[98]

	Starchy Roots	Vegetable Oils	Vegetables	Fruit
■ Imports 1961	567	383	918	2498
▨ Imports 1968	1022	565	1137	2830
▢ Imports 1978	1406	616	978	2743
◩ Imports 1988	1381	903	2041	4041
☐ Imports 1998	1566	1115	2915	5382

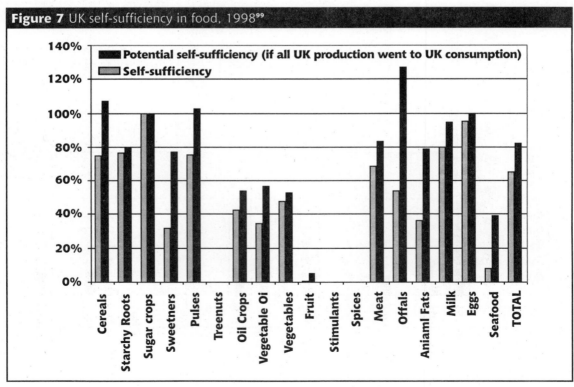

Figure 7 UK self-sufficiency in food, 1998[99]

In 1980 the UK trade gap in food, feed and drink was £3.5 billion, which increased to £5.9 billion in 1990 and to £8.3 billion in 1999. British farmers now rely on export markets at the same time as food supply in the UK is reliant on ever increasing levels of imports for many products that could be sourced in the UK.

In many cases countries import and export similar quantities of the same food products.[100] This may seem like an illogical situation, and in many instances it is. A recent report has highlighted the instances in which countries import and export large quantities of particular foodstuffs.[101] For example, in the UK in 1997, 126 million litres of liquid milk was imported into the UK and at the same time 270 million litres of milk was exported from the UK. 23,000 tonnes of milk powder was imported into the UK and 153,000 tonnes exported.[102] UK milk imports have doubled over the last 20 years, but there has been a four-fold increase in UK milk exports over the last 30 years.[103]

Despite this, there is now intense pressure to further liberalise trade in foodstuffs. In World Trade Organisation (WTO) negotiations, the Cairns Group is seeking to remove barriers to international trade in food and agricultural subsidies. This Group, comprising agricultural exporting nations, including Argentina, Egypt, New Zealand, Brazil and Australia argue that production and export subsidies, quotas and tariffs should be removed.

3.4.2 Is organic food trade any better?

"Over 80 per cent of organic food sold in the UK comes from abroad. This may be acceptable for tropical fruits, which can't realistically be produced here, but temperate vegetable and fruit should surely be home-grown" Alan and Jackie Gear of the Henry Doubleday Research Association.[104]

Many people believe that it is a long-standing absurdity that Britain has to import over three-quarters of its organic produce, and that despite consumer demand, only two per cent of its land is organically farmed.[105] Section 5.2 provides an overview of the sector and the energy consumed through organic imports. For all product categories, apart from eggs, imports constituted a significant proportion of supplies in 1999/2000 (**Table 4**). Organic meat imports, which were negligible in 1997/1998 increased to 30 per cent of sales in 1999/2000 and over the same period imports of dairy products rose from 10 to 40 per cent.

The supply of organic foodstuffs has come to rely even more heavily on global sourcing, for example, over three-quarters of all organic fruit and vegetables, cereals and baked products, multi-ingredient products and beverages are imported.

Perhaps of most significance is the fact that UK self-sufficiency in organic fruit, vegetables and herbs has fallen to 15 per cent. This was the most lucrative product category in 1999/2000 with sales amounting to £230 million, 38 per cent of the total organic market.

Table 4 UK retail sales and imports of the main organic food product categories[106]

	1997 / 1998		1998 / 1999		1999 / 2000	
	UK sales (£m)	Imports (%)	UK sales (£m)	Imports (%)	UK sales (£m)	Imports (%)
Eggs	5	N/s	9	0	31	0
Meat	13	0	14	5	24	30
Dairy	18	10	54	40	106	40
Babyfoods	8	N/s	12	70	24	65
Cereals and baked products	36	50	50	70	67	75
Multi-ingredient	18	20	58	80	97	80
Fruit, vegetables and herbs	140	80	175	82	230	85
Beverages	16	N/s	18	90	24	85

Up until 1999 the multiple retailers concentrated their efforts on marketing fresh fruit and vegetables and were yet to offer a comprehensive range of organically produced meat products. With this in mind it is interesting to note that in 1999, 82 per cent of the organic fruit and vegetables consumed in the UK were imported whereas organic meat imports stood at 5 per cent. The following year, imports rose to 30 per cent when the supermarkets became involved in marketing organic meat. It could be said that high levels of imports are inevitable in the short term when UK demand cannot be met by UK producers. This situation could change in the longer term, as one retailer claims:

"Sainsbury's has to import to meet the ever growing demand in the UK. However, by doing this it is helping to establish the UK organic market. Sainsbury's hopes that British farmers will eventually make this market their own, substituting with home grown products where they can."

However, this situation may not be fulfilled.

"With the entry of these (multinational) companies, plus the appearance of volume private label producers, the organic market is looking a little more like its conventional counterpart" The Soil Association, 2001.[107]

The ability of supermarkets to supply a wide range of products all year round at stores located across Britain, rests on them being able to secure large volumes of uniform produce to a predictable schedule and to specific product packaging and labelling requirements. These demands often preclude smaller producers. The 1997 European Fresh Produce Convention heard predictions from experts that each retailer would limit its preferred distributors to 'no more than three per commodity group', in other words only three suppliers of tomatoes, cauliflower, etc.[108] This would severely restrict any attempts to use small, local suppliers. Additionally, if overseas producers can meet supermarkets' criteria and at a lower price, then organic and non-organic foodstuffs are likely to continue to be imported in large quantities.

UK imports of non-organic fruit increased by 90 per cent between 1968 and 1998 and over the same period vegetable imports grew by 156 per cent. **Figure 8** shows that there has been a close correlation between increases in imports of conventionally produced fruit and vegetables and the emergence of the multiple retailers.

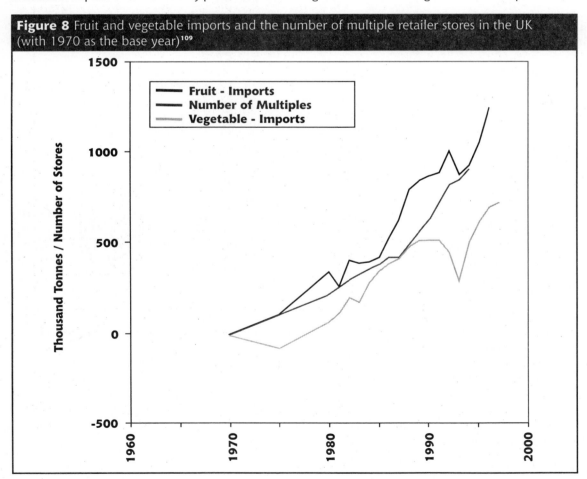

Figure 8 Fruit and vegetable imports and the number of multiple retailer stores in the UK (with 1970 as the base year)[109]

The consequence has been a decline in domestic fruit production to the point where even if all the UK's home-grown fruit was consumed domestically, the UK could at present be only 5 per cent self-sufficient in fruit.

In the dairy sector domestic production has also been damaged. International competitiveness and price wars between the main supermarkets, have exerted continuous downward pressure on milk prices. Small dairy farmers are struggling to survive. A recent Panorama programme on BBC television considered the future of farming in the UK following the foot and mouth epidemic and interviewed a conventional dairy farmer, Mike Edwards, who has 65 Brown Swiss cows on only 100 acres of land. He stated that:

"At the end of the day there are only four or five major supermarkets. Really they can just do what the hell they like with the price of milk and there's very little we can do to stop it, and we're at the stage now where every litre of milk we send off we're making about 2 or 3 pence a litre loss. We just can't sustain that." [110]

The Edwards family now, in effect, subsidise the milk they produce. In order to keep the farm going, both parents do other jobs. Mike Edwards now works part-time in Tesco which sells milk at 46p a litre while he gets 18p (May/April 2001).[111] Even outside the dairy sector the profit margin for farmers that supply the supermarkets has in many instances become negligible and some are selling their produce at prices lower than the costs of production (**Figure 9**).

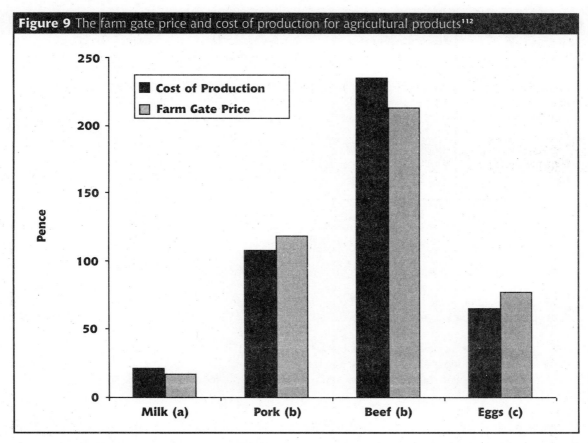

Figure 9 The farm gate price and cost of production for agricultural products[112]

Notes: The figures are based on averages of current costs/prices and in reality may be subject to some slight variation.
   (a) price per litre
   (b) price per kilogram (based on 23/24 month old spring-born calves in the case of beef)
   (c) price per dozen large free range eggs.

Could this experience be repeated in the organic sector? Some argue that it will. For example, when the Soil Association surveyed wholesalers and packers some said "sourcing from overseas was often easier than encouraging UK producers to convert." [113]

"If organic farming is captured by the big supermarket chains, it will soon begin to look like conventional farming, just without the pesticides and fertilisers. Yet it can be so much more, a powerful force for ecological, economic and cultural renewal. If this role is to be sustained, local trading networks and shops such as Out of this World must uphold the high organic standards that the big superstores will try to undermine" George Monbiot.[114]

The market share of local independent organic marketing schemes has declined in recent years.[115] If the multiple retailers continue to source organic foods anywhere they are cheaper to produce than in the UK, imports will increase and localised direct marketing, together with small-scale organic producers will suffer.

In the case of fruit and vegetables, the Soil Association expects the conversion of larger producers to help the development of the home market. However, although large-scale organic production will benefit the supermarkets, it could lead to practices that require high levels of external inputs and mechanisation. Moreover, if conversion is not accompanied with diversification and large organic farms produce only a few crops, there will be a significant environmental impact associated with distribution. The average size of organic holdings in the UK, at 146 hectares, is already over three times that of organic farms in Denmark and eight times larger than the average organic farm in Austria (**Table 5**).

Table 5 Organic retail sales, area and average size of holdings in Europe[116]

	Organic retail sales (£/capita/year)	Organic and in-conversion land area (hectares/1000 capita)	Average area of organic holdings (hectares)
Austria	25.00	45.0	18
Italy	10.53	16.9	19
Holland	9.35	1.8	22
France	8.47	5.4	38
Germany	19.51	5.5	43
Denmark	45.28	30.1	44
UK	10.25	7.1	146

The post-farm gate environmental impact associated with organic produce is receiving more. The main areas of concern are the:

- Increasing distance between producer and consumer due to increasing organic imports and the centralised distribution systems of UK multiple retailers;
- processing of organic food and drink and the emergence of organic ready-to-eat meals; and
- packaging of organic foodstuffs.

Several commentators, some from within the organic movement, have expressed concerns about processed and packaged organic foods and organic food miles. Several years ago, Lawrence Woodward, David Fleming and Hardy Vogtmann were beginning to see a move away from the founding principles of the international organic movement:

"Highly processed organic food is likely to be as nutritionally deficient as highly processed conventional foods. Out of season production, lengthy distribution chains and over-packaging of organic produce have the same environmental and social consequences as those which are produced by conventional methods. The extent to which the movement has moved away from the founding concept of health can be seen in the views espoused by some that the organic sector will have succeeded when an organic Mars Bar is on sale. The only thing that has really been remembered is the prohibition of 'chemical intervention'." [117]

More recently, Alan and Jackie Gear of the Henry Doubleday Research Association stated that:

"Organic proponents are on weaker ground when it comes to issues like transport and food processing. It is hard to make the case for organic food being the most environmentally friendly when it is transported thousands of miles....." [118]

3.4.3 The environmental efficiency of different forms of transport

Table 6 gives an indication of the environmental efficiency of the different forms of freight transport. In terms of carbon dioxide emissions there are significant differences between freight distribution by ship, which results in 10 to 40 grammes of carbon dioxide emissions per tonne-kilometre, and the 570 to 1580 grammes of carbon dioxide emissions per tonne-kilometre resulting from airfreight.

A rough comparison of different modes of transport for inter-continental freight transport shows that distribution by road produces six times more carbon dioxide than shipping and that distributing products by plane results in 50 times more carbon dioxide than sea freight. The increases in international trade by plane are therefore of particular concern.

Table 6 Emissions and energy use by different modes of freight transport[119]

Mode	Description	CO2 Emissions (grammes CO2/tonne-kilometre)	Energy Consumption (MJ/tonne-kilometre)
Air	Short-haul Long-haul	1580 570	23.7 8.5
Road	Transit Van Medium Truck Large Truck	97 85 63	1.7 1.5 1.1
Ship	Roll-on/roll-off Bulk carrier	40 10	0.55 0.15

Although often overlooked in analyses of the food system, shopping is also a food miles issue.[120] A shopping trip of 8 kilometres in an average sized petrol car, in which 30 kilograms of food is purchased, results in the same quantity of carbon dioxide emissions as transporting that produce 952 kilometres by lorry and 38 kilometres by plane in a short-haul flight (**Tables 6 and 7**). This reveals the significance of all transport involved in the movement of food products from origin to the consumer. Different retail and marketing options can influence the distance, mode of transport and environmental impact of shopping trips. Home delivery fruit and vegetable box schemes avoid car use and when retail outlets are located in town and city centres, with easy access by bicycle, on foot or public transport, the proportion of shopping trips by car is reduced.[121 122] However, supermarkets, particularly when situated out-of-town, want consumers to arrive by car, as they are likely to purchase more goods than when shopping on foot or by public transport.[123]

Table 7 Emissions and energy use by car travel[124]

Car Description		CO2 Emissions (g/km)	Energy Consumption (MJ/km)	Fuel Consumption (litres/km)
Petrol	Small Medium Large	170 220 270	2.5 3.3 4.0	0.074 0.095 0.117
Diesel	Small Medium	120 140	1.7 2.0	0.045 0.052

Very few studies have investigated the environmental impact of the transport components of food supply chains. This is surprising, given that the distance between producer and consumer or food miles has increased significantly in recent decades. Food supply has also become increasingly complicated and more transport-intensive due to increases in the three main areas of transportation in the food system associated with: international trade; road freight distribution in the UK; and shopping trips by car. These three generators of food miles are described in the following sections.

3.4.4 The problems of international freight transport

Trade-related transportation is one of the fastest growing sources of greenhouse gas emissions and is therefore significant in terms of climate change and efforts to cut emission levels.[125] In 1992 trade related transportation accounted for almost 7 per cent of fossil fuel related carbon dioxide emissions. International freight transport associated with world trade is expected to increase by 70 per cent between 1992 and 2004 from 29 to 49 trillion tonne-kilometres.[126] If this occurs then the carbon dioxide emissions resulting from international trade will increase from approximately 1.45 billion tonnes in 1992 to 2.45 billion tonnes in 2004.

One study has estimated that UK imports of food products and animal feed involved transportation by sea, air and road amounting to over 83 billion tonne-kilometres.[127] This required 1.6 billion litres of fuel and, based on a conservative figure of 50 grammes of carbon dioxide per tonne-kilometre (see **Table 6**), resulted in 4.1 million tonnes of carbon dioxide emissions. In terms of tonne-kilometres this was double the figure for food freight movements within Britain.

Food on the sea

Between 1965 and 1999, UK overseas sea-borne trade doubled to reach 388 million tonnes.[128] In 1999, approximately half (47.5 per cent) of all UK sea-borne trade was in fossil fuels (including crude petroleum, petroleum products, coal and gas) and of this 40 per cent consisted of imports.[129] In addition to imports and exports, oil cargoes also constitute a high proportion (around 65 to 70 per cent) of the total freight carried by UK coastal shipping.[130]

Food, drink and agricultural inputs at 18.6 million tonnes made up 29 per cent of all UK non-fuel bulk sea-borne trade in 1999.

Food on the road

Although most UK imports and exports are carried by ship, transportation of UK imports between the source and port of departure (and port of arrival and the destination for exports) is often by lorry. In many instances the lorry distances will be greater than shipping distance. This is particularly true for UK trade with Southern and Eastern Europe by truck and ferry across the Channel. There have been massive increases in road freight movements between the UK and the Continent and Ireland in recent decades.[131] Roll-On Roll-Off (Ro-Ro) ferries transport the majority of these road goods vehicles (RGVs) which now account for around 14 per cent of total UK port freight traffic, having grown by some 51 per cent between 1991 and 1999. In 1999, UK trade with continental Europe by road amounted to 15.9 million tonnes, which was transported an average distance of 1060 kilometres, amounting to 16 billion tonnes-kilometres.[132] Foodstuffs and agricultural products accounted for about 27 per cent of the total in terms of the quantity (4.4 million tonnes) and the distance moved (4.1 billion tonne-kilometres), resulting in approximately 258 thousand tonnes of carbon dioxide **(Figure 10)**.

Imports and exports of agricultural and food products by road increased by 90 per cent between 1989 and 1999 and the distance that these products are moved increased by 51 per cent.

In 1999, 839,000 RGVs passed through the Channel Tunnel; the combined Ro-Ro ferry and Channel Tunnel traffic to the Continent was just under 6.6 million RGV units, about three times larger than in 1982 and 71 per cent higher than in 1990. The Irish Sea trade has also grown rapidly in recent years. The number of trucks carrying freight, that are transported by sea, between Britain and Ireland trebled between 1982 and 1999 and there has been particularly rapid growth since 1993.[133]

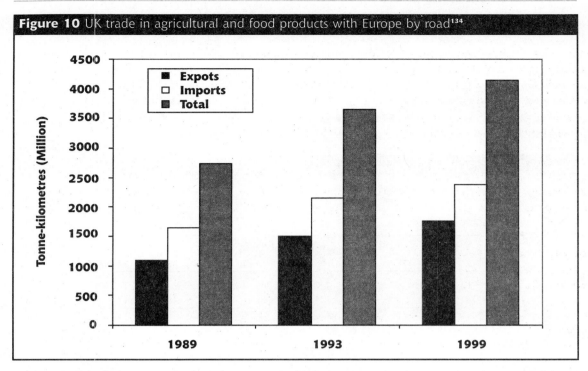

Figure 10 UK trade in agricultural and food products with Europe by road[134]

Increases in road freight movements within the European Union, are a direct result of the introduction of a completely liberalised (or deregulated) 'single market' in 1991, that permitted the free movement of road freight across national borders within the EU. The Maastricht Treaty established a Cohesion Fund to provide a financial contribution to create a Trans-European Road Network (TERN) to ensure the efficiency of the internal market, by improving the mobility of people and goods, and to reinforce economic cohesion. The TERN plans to add 12,000 kilometres of motorway specifically intended for road freight, which involves a total of 50,000 kilometres of new roads. It aims to increase trade in the European Single Market by building up routes for lorry traffic, filling in 'missing links', relieving bottlenecks and linking up peripheral member states with the rest of Europe. This decision to create a Europe-wide motorway network and encourage Southern European states to trade their products across the EU has inevitably resulted in a significant expansion in road freight and particularly in long-distance truck movements.

It is not surprising that the European Environment Agency (EEA) states that "transport in the EU is becoming less not more environmentally sustainable" in its 2001 annual report on the sector.[135] The executive director of the EEA has stressed that progress is "imperative" if the EU is to approach its 2010 target to decouple transport growth from economic growth, although the report states that such decoupling for freight transport is unlikely. Under new guidelines for funding trans-European transport networks, the EU sustainable development strategy calls for priority funding for public transport, railways and inland waterways. The European Commission also intends to propose a framework ensuring that by 2004 the price of using different modes of transport *better reflects costs to society.*[136]

Food in the air

Although most food is distributed by road and ship, the airfreight of foodstuffs is increasing. World airfreight has expanded significantly in recent decades to reach 100 billion tonne-kilometres in 1998.[137] Aviation accounts for 12 per cent of global transport carbon dioxide emissions and although the emissions of individual aircraft continue to fall, total carbon dioxide emissions are expected to triple over the next three decades.[138] The IPCC estimate that aviation is responsible for 3.5 per cent of man made climate change. Scientists also predict that the indirect effect on the enhanced greenhouse effect of aircraft nitrogen oxides emissions might be as high as that of carbon dioxide emissions.[139] Aircraft emissions of soot, water vapor and sulphates are also thought to have a significant impact, with the latter contributing to the formation of cirrus clouds which have quite a significant greenhouse impact.[140] The Royal Commission on Environmental Pollution has estimated that, due to increases in aircraft greenhouse gas emissions, the contribution of aviation to man-made global warming will increase fivefold between 1992 and 2050.[141]

UK imports of fish products and fruit and vegetables by plane increased by 240 per cent and 90 per cent, respectively, between 1980 and 1990.[142] In the period 1980 to 1998 UK airfreight imports of fruit and vegetables more than trebled (**Figure 11**). Of all UK imports by plane in 1998, fruit and vegetables made up the largest commodity category and stood at 13 per cent of airfreight imports by weight.[143]

Total UK air freight (imports and exports) doubled in the decade to 1999, to reach 2 million tonnes, and is expected to increase at a rate of 7.5 per cent a year to 2010.[144] Such a trend is potentially highly damaging, volatile and is ultimately unsustainable.

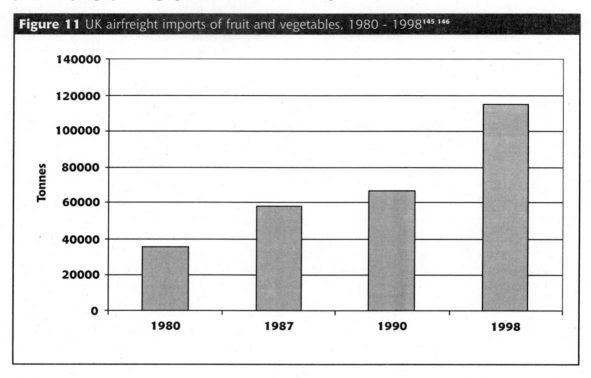

Figure 11 UK airfreight imports of fruit and vegetables, 1980 - 1998[145][146]

The UK airfreight industry is dominated by the London airports, and by Heathrow Airport in particular, which handles more than four times more freight than its nearest rival, Gatwick. In 1999, almost 60 per cent of all UK airfreight, over 1.2 million tonnes, passed through Heathrow and between 1989 and 1999 the amount of freight handled by Heathrow almost doubled.[147] Considering this increase and the proportion of airfreight passing through Heathrow, it is not surprising that there are proposals for new runways and perhaps a totally new two runway airport in the South East.[148] Local opposition to airports and airport expansion is increasing due to concerns about noise, air pollution and the loss of countryside. Although modern aircraft engines are quieter, their emissions on the ground, particularly nitrogen oxides, have increased.[149]

Not only are greenhouse gas emissions from international airfreight and shipping excluded from international agreements such as the Kyoto Protocol, but fuel for aircraft and ships is also exempt from fuel tax and value added tax. Motorists pay about 80p for a litre of unleaded petrol (in November 2000), comprising a basic cost of 20p with about 48p in excise duty and 12p in VAT. However airlines pay about 18p per litre of fuel.[150]

Although the 1998 Transport White Paper stated that *"aviation should meet the external costs, including environmental costs, which it imposes"*, no action has yet been taken. The UK Treasury has calculated that if excise duty was paid (but not VAT) on aviation fuel at the same rate as unleaded petrol this would raise £5 billion a year.[151] The European Parliament is now backing EU Commission proposals for an EU-wide aviation emissions charge and aviation taxes.[152][153]

3.4.5 The national food mile

As a sector of the UK economy, food, drink and tobacco were responsible for a 33 per cent increase in energy consumed through road freight distribution between 1985 and 1995.[154] Between 1978 and 1999, UK domestic use of food, feed and drink increased by 9 per cent, while the amount of food products being distributed around the country increased by 16 per cent. Significantly, the distance that these foodstuffs were transported within the UK increased by over 50 per cent over this period (**Table 8**).[155] Additionally, the proportion of empty lorries on the roads remains significant, at around 30 per cent, and has been broadly static for the last 10 years, despite industry efforts to reduce such wasted journeys.[156]

In the UK in 1998, the transport involved in food-related commodities (agricultural products, live animals, foodstuffs, animal fodder, and fertiliser) amounted to 48.8 billion tonne-kilometres, around a third of all commodity movement by road in the UK.[157] This resulted in approximately 4 million tonnes of carbon dioxide emissions.

Additionally, other commodity groups supply inputs to various stages in food supply chains, including metal products to farms and the packaging industry; chemicals to produce pesticides and plastics; petroleum products; and machinery. If these factors are considered, the food system could account for up to 40 per cent of all UK road freight.[158] Over 98 per cent of all movements of foodstuffs are by road, compared to the average for all commodity groups of 65 per cent.[159]

One reason for a large proportion of food products being transported by lorry, rather than by environmentally less damaging modes, is the multiple retailers' reliance on road transportation which is reflected in the location of many regional distribution centres (RDC's) adjacent to the motorway network.

Table 8 Tonnage and distance travelled by food 1978-98 in the UK[160]

	Quantity (millions of tonnes)	Average distance (kilometres)
1978	**287**	**82**
1983	**264**	**89**
1988	**302**	**100**
1993	**300**	**119**
1998	**346**	**123**
1999	**333**	**125**

3.4.6 The shopper food mile

There have also been increases in the number of shopping trips by car and the distance travelled per year shopping for food. Between 1985/86 and 1996/98 there was a 57 per cent increase in the distance of car shopping trips, from an average of 14 to 22 kilometres per person per week.[161] Over the same period there were increases in the average number of shopping journeys by car per person per week from 1.68 to 2.42 and in the average distance of each shopping trip from 8.3 to 9.1 kilometres. A large increase in the number of out-of-town stores and the closure of many small local shops over the last 20 years are two important factors that have influenced these trends.[162] The example in **Box 3** shows the carbon dioxide emissions associated with shopping trips of various distances and **Table 13** summarises other pollutant emissions as a result of shopping by car.

Box 3 Examples of carbon dioxide emissions from household activities and shopping trips

Table 9 Household activities[163]

	CO2 (Kg)
Space Heating	1506
Hot Water	864
Cooking	125
Pump and fans	96
Lights and appliances	1650
Total	**4241**

Table 10 Electrical appliances

	Energy Consumed (kWh)	CO2 (g)
Boil a kettle full of water	0.093	40
Operate a 100W light for 1 hour	0.100	43

Table 11 The carbon dioxide emissions associated with shopping trips of different distances

CAR	Description	CO2 Emission (kg)	
		Average (8.3km)	**Maximum (70km)**
Petrol	Small	1.4	12.0
	Medium	1.8	15.4
Diesel	Large	2.2	19.0
	Small	1.0	8.4
	Medium	1.2	10.0

In 1997/99 the average shopping trip by car was 8.3 kilometres.[164] The carbon dioxide emissions associated with a journey of this distance range from 1 kilogram in the case of a small diesel car to 2.2 kilograms in a large petrol car. In the case of the latter, the same amount of carbon dioxide is emitted as when operating a 100 watt lightbulb for over 51 hours.

However, the '20-minute catchment area' is a well established technique used by planners employed by the multiple retailers to determine which sites will be most profitable for their stores. They take a map of an area and draw a 20-minute 'isochrone' around the site. Within this area, people can drive to the supermarket within 20 minutes. The more fast roads there are in the locality, the larger the area will be inside the isochrone - and the farther people will have to drive. The planners calculate that people will drive up to 35 kilometres, and back, just to go shopping.[165] Based on this maximum distance of 70 kilometres, a shopping trip in a large petrol car would result in 19 kilograms of carbon dioxide emissions. This is equivalent to the carbon dioxide emissions from a power station, resulting from boiling a kettle full of water 475 times.

Research has demonstrated that people are concerned about climate change and want to help to cut emissions. Yet that same research indicates that people are not aware of the link between their use of energy in the home and climate change.[166] The Government has set out to inform people about that link in the 'are you doing your bit?' campaign and to provide further incentives to individuals to act through the Energy Saving Trust's 'energy efficiency marketing campaign'. Similarly, the European Commission is to launch a public awareness raising campaign and a series of targets for low-energy buildings and households' use of low-energy appliances and lightbulbs.[167]

Unfortunately, there have been no similar government schemes aimed at raising awareness, influencing consumer behaviour, and altering purchasing patterns to reduce the environmental damage caused by food miles, and consumers have not been encouraged to purchase 'low-transport' foodstuffs. This applies to the transportation involved in distributing products to the point of sale and also in relation to each marketing system and the transport options for shopping.

4) Eating oil: The risks

In the countries that are most dependent on oil, reserves are at their lowest. Less than 2 per cent of known reserves are in Western Europe. Two-thirds of oil reserves lie in the Middle East, and concerns remain that the political situation in the region could translate into an abrupt increase in price or shortfall in supply. Since 1973 there have been oil crises in 1980, 1991 and 2000, when oil prices doubled or trebled over a short period of time. On all four occasions oil prices have increased due events in the Middle East. Apart from these concerns about crude oil prices and disruptions in supply, the threat of global warming and climate change means that it is now more essential than ever that we move away from our dependency on fossil fuels.

4.1 Oil is a finite resource

"The 1973 oil crisis took us by surprise, causing sudden panic...Are we in danger of experiencing another world oil crisis like that of 1973 - which quadrupled the price of oil, unleashed a wave of high inflation, and turned the world upside down?" Anthony Simpson author of *The Seven Sisters*, which looked at the oil industry.[168]

A fundamental driver of economic activity in the 20th century was an abundant supply of cheap oil. At first it came largely from the USA, but discovery peaked around 1930, leading to a corresponding peak in production some forty years later. The focus of supply then shifted to the Middle East, as international oil companies tapped its vast resources. However, oil companies soon lost their control in a series of expropriations as the host governments sought a greater share of the proceeds.[169] In the early 1970s western nations, particularly the USA, were consuming oil in increasing quantities, and becoming still more dependent on foreign producers, led by Saudi Arabia.[170] In 1973, some Middle East governments, by boycotting exports to the West, used their control of oil as a weapon in their conflict with Israel over its occupation of Palestine, giving rise to the first oil shock.

Colin J. Campbell describes the situation in *The Coming Oil Crisis*: "The oil shocks of the 1970s were short-lived because there were then plenty of new oil and gas finds to bring onstream. This time there are virtually no new prolific basins to yield a crop of giant fields sufficient to have a global impact. The growing Middle East control of the market is likely to lead to a radical and permanent increase in the price of oil, before physical shortages begin to appear within the first decade of the 21st century. The world's economy has been driven by an abundant supply of cheap oil-based energy for the best part of this century. The coming oil crisis will accordingly be an economic and political discontinuity of historic proportions, as the world adjusts to a new energy environment"[171]

During the 1970s, Organisation of Petroleum Exporting Countries (OPEC) states reined their production while other countries were producing oil at full capacity. The subsequent crises of 1973, 1980 and 1991 could be explained by supply constraints (**Figure 12**). Oil prices tripled more recently, in just 20 months between January 1999 and September 2000, as demand for energy outstripped supply. In addition to OPEC quota restrictions which explain the supply constraints in late 2000, it is important to note that the OPEC countries, mainly in the Middle East account for 40 per cent of world oil production.[172] The Middle East is a strategic factor in the contemporary oil market. Consumer countries have to consider this carefully as the Arab countries are about to reach their production peak in a few years.[173] Additionally, concerns have been expressed that the basic ingredients of a crisis in the Middle East remain in place, as they were in 1973.[174]

Oil prices reached a ten-year high in October 2000. Brent crude prices surged from about $32 a barrel to above $35 and anxiety that Iraq could cut its exports sent the price even higher on New York's NYMEX exchange, at one point reaching $37 per barrel, not far from the $42 peak when Saddam Hussein set fire to Kuwait's oilfields in 1990.[175] Iraq, which is the fourth largest OPEC producer at 2.6 million barrels per day, has periodically used the threat of an export embargo to negotiate a lifting of UN sanctions. It is also possible that OPEC could once again intervene in the Israeli-Palestinian conflict, using oil as a weapon.

Following the destruction of the World Trade Centre in New York on 11th September 2001, Brent crude oil prices rose $4 a barrel to more than $31 a barrel. However, in the days that followed, prices slipped back to about $26 a barrel on predictions that weaker demand for oil, particularly aviation fuel, would be more important than any possible disruptions to supply. In the long term, however, disruptions will lead to sustained price rises.[177]

Only Saudi Arabia and Iraq have the power to have a significant impact on oil supplies. Saudi Arabia currently produces more than eight million barrels a day but has the capacity to increase output by some 1.7 million barrels and to do so within just two months. In recent years, the tightness of supply and demand in the oil market

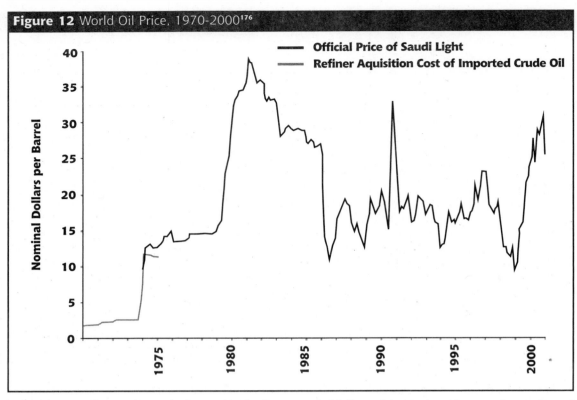

Figure 12 World Oil Price, 1970-2000[176]

Note: the price data are in nominal terms i.e. the figures are in 'dollars-of-the-day' and have not been adjusted for inflation.

has brought the Saudis back into the role of 'swing producer', a role in which they came to prominence in the 1970s but lost as production in Russia, the North Sea and other non-OPEC regions grew.

4.1.1 The end of the 'cheap and abundant oil' era: consumption does lead to depletion

"*For the last thirty years there has been abundant good information that oil production would peak and start to go into decline around the turn of the century. The failure to listen to these warnings has left the UK (and all other nations) totally unprepared for the consequences of the oil shock which will take place during the first decade of (21st) century, with the result that the shock, when it comes, will be catastrophic… The procession of unheeded warnings has continued. Individual energy analysts have produced detailed empirical studies showing that the turning point for oil would occur around the turn of the century. It is evident, that one of the reasons for this surreal situation, with imminent and devastating change unrecognised by the experts and discounted by government, is that the problem falls outside the mind-set of market economics. Expertise, it seems, wipes the mind clean of commonsense. Maybe, for a moment, we should stop thinking, and just feel the reality of energy famines*" David Fleming.[182]

Discovery of oil and gas peaked in the 1960s. Production is set to peak too, with five Middle East countries regaining control of world supply.[178] Almost two-thirds of the world's total reserves of crude oil are located in the Middle East. Outside Western Europe, which ranks last among the world's oil producing regions (2 per cent or less of total oil reserves), the remainder of the world's potential crude oil supply splits almost evenly (with estimates of 4.2-8.7 per cent) between the other regions: North America, Africa, Central and South America, Eastern Europe and the former Soviet Union, and the Far East and Oceania.[179]

In The Coming Oil Crisis, Colin J. Campbell, an industry expert, makes an assessment of future world oil supply by considering how much conventional oil remains to be produced, and its depletion pattern. Between 1980 and 1998 there was a 11.2 per cent increase in world crude oil production, from 59.6 to 66.9 million barrels of oil per day.[180] Current world production rates are about 25 Gb (billion barrels) per year (**Figure 13**).

A simple calculation shows that if consumption levels remain constant, world crude oil reserves, at approximately 1 trillion barrels, could be exhausted around 2040. [181]

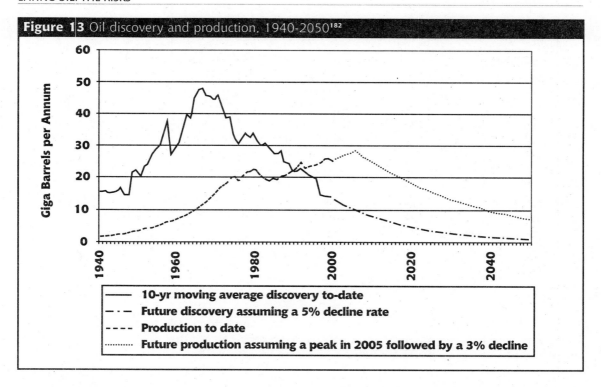

Figure 13 Oil discovery and production, 1940-2050[182]

Legend:
— 10-yr moving average discovery to-date
— · — Future discovery assuming a 5% decline rate
- - - - Production to date
············ Future production assuming a peak in 2005 followed by a 3% decline

The level of what is commonly called "reserves" or "proved reserves" is critical for a finite resource such as crude oil. Various scientists have tried to describe the depletion process of a non-renewable resource. The most convincing theoretical model was set in 1959 by the American geologist Dr. M. King Hubbert. Hubbert drew a bell shaped curve to describe the trend of production in the southern USA. In America, according to Hubbert's estimates the mid point was reached in 1960. In the UK and Norway the crest was attained in 1999 and the Middle East would reach the climax in 2010.[183] UK oil reserves are expected to be depleted by 2010.[184] Hubbert's theory has proved itself by empirical evidence.

At the same time OECD countries are being overtaken as the major consumers of oil by expanding economies such as in Asia. In 1985, Asia accounted for 18 per cent of world oil consumption, which increased to 26.4 per cent in 1997. Oil consumption in the region surpassed Europe in 1992 and exceeded total U.S. consumption in 1994.

According to Exxon, Asia will consume more crude oil than the U.S. and Europe combined sometime between 2005 and 2010. Asia is destined to become the world's top oil guzzler in the not-to-distant future.[185]

The three main purposes for which oil is used worldwide are food, transport and heating. In the near future the competition for oil for these three activities will be raw and real. An energy famine is likely to affect poorer countries first, when increases in the cost of paraffin, used for cooking, place it beyond their reach. Following the peak in production, food supplies all over the world will begin to be disrupted, not only because of price increases but because the oil will no longer be there.[182]

4.2 Stormy weather: the evidence and impact of climate change

"Once scientists used to refer to the effects of global warming being bad for our grandchildren. Five years ago they began to talk about our children, and now we are already seeing the effects… Last winter's floods in the UK were openly ascribed to a change in weather caused by global warming. It could have been a fluke coinciding with predictions – but one flood in a 100 years can now be expected every five or ten years, or possibly more often" Paul Brown, Environmental Correspondent, The Guardian.[186]

Man made climate change, which is a sign of the unsustainable nature of human activity, is caused by emissions of greenhouse gases, particularly carbon dioxide (CO_2) from burning fossil fuels (**Figure 14**).[187] During the last decade the evidence of a link between anthropogenic emissions of greenhouse gases, concentrations of these gases in the atmosphere and average global temperatures has been increasing. Climate science has developed 'backwards and forwards'.[188] The analysis of ancient ice cores and tree rings in Greenland and the Antarctic has allowed calculations of the composition of the atmosphere before records began. This data, together with current observations of rising temperatures and greenhouse gas emissions has been entered into sophisticated computer models that have been developed to predict the effects of emissions on the climate in the future. The scientists have made significant progress in improving the certainty of their calculations:

- Global temperatures are rising faster than ever before recorded, and as a result weather patterns are becoming less predictable and more extreme.[189] Temperatures have risen by 0.6°C in the last century.
- Since 1750 the concentration of carbon dioxide in the atmosphere has risen by 31 per cent to the highest level in millions of years.[190]
- Ice now covers 15 per cent less of the arctic ocean than it did 20 years ago. In places the Arctic permafrost is melting which could aggravate the greenhouse effect by allowing the release of huge amounts of carbon at present locked up in the frozen soil.[191]
- The 1990s was the warmest decade since instrument records began in 1861, and 1998 was the hottest year ever recorded. Experience in the UK backs this up. In England, four of the five warmest years in a 340-year record have been in the 1990s and 1999 was the joint warmest year ever.[192]

The Intergovernmental Panel on Climate Change, an international advisory group consisting of 2,500 of the world's leading climate change experts, recently stated that "the balance of evidence suggests that there is a discernible human influence on global climate."[193]

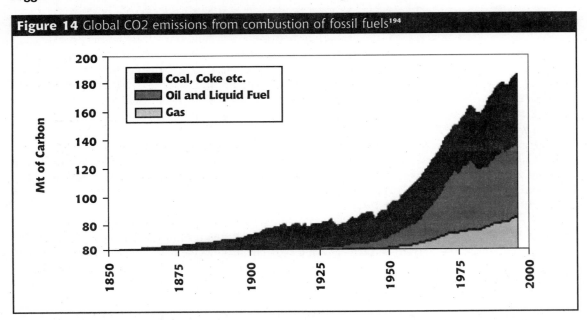

Figure 14 Global CO2 emissions from combustion of fossil fuels[194]

4.2.1 Climate change: the source of greenhouse gas emissions

World carbon dioxide emissions from the consumption of fossil fuels increased by 21 per cent between 1980 and 1999, from 18.8 to 22.9 billion tonnes.[195] The Intergovernmental Panel on Climate Change (IPCC) has recommended cuts of 60-80 per cent in greenhouse gases to stabilise atmospheric levels of CO2 at the existing artificially high level.[196] In Bonn in 2001, 186 countries including 37 industrialised nations agreed to the Kyoto Protocol, which will cut emissions by an average of one to three per cent. The USA, which is responsible for a quarter of the world's greenhouse gas emissions, made no commitment to reductions. The EU will now start turning the treaty into law for all member countries, forcing a cut in greenhouse gas emissions of eight per cent on 1990 levels by 2010 (**Box 4**).

Box 4 Political failure to tackle climate change

Internal European Commission disagreements over a future carbon dioxide emissions trading scheme delayed the planned approval of a major EU package of climate change measures in October 2001.[197] Environment commissioner Margot Wallström wants very limited exemptions, while enterprise commissioner Erkki Liikanen is fighting for firms to be able to opt out much more freely. This is an example of the conflict between improved environmental protection and continued economic growth which often translates into a business as usual approach. The measures should have included proposals to ratify the Kyoto Protocol and for new steps to cut greenhouse gases based on recommendations from the European climate change programme (ECCP). As a result the Kyoto Protocol will not come into force until 2002 at the earliest.[198] Margot Wallström has also expressed disappointment that EU heads of government had "missed an opportunity for political leadership" in the failure to endorse a proposal for the EU to commit to specified cuts in greenhouse gases beyond the Kyoto Protocol 'first commitment period' of 2008-12.[199]

The UK's reduction target under the Kyoto Protocol will be 12.5 per cent, allowing for lower reductions in poorer EU member states. The UK has a separate goal to reduce carbon dioxide emissions by 20 per cent by 2010 and is one of the few industrialised countries to meet the Rio target to return their greenhouse gas emissions to 1990 levels by 2000. However, this was largely due to a shift to the use of natural gas in power stations and reduced industrial activity, particularly manufacturing. Although UK carbon dioxide emissions are falling at the moment, they are expected to begin rising again.[200] The UK government believe that industrialised country emissions may have to be reduced by more than the 60-70 per cent that will ultimately be required globally; reductions of as much as 90 per cent may be required.[201] Reductions on this scale would require a significant shift away from the use of fossil fuels as an energy source, even phasing them out completely and would be based on a global agreement for 'contraction and convergence' which sets an upper limit for the carbon dioxide concentration in the atmosphere of 550 parts per million by volume (ppmv) - double the pre-industrial level - and a convergence date of 2050.[202] This would actually mean a substantial increase (of almost 50 per cent) in atmospheric carbon dioxide levels as the current concentration is 370 ppmv.

Currently, the highest emitting fifth of the world's population contributes 63 per cent of documented CO2 emissions, while the lowest emitting fifth emits just 2 per cent.[203] In 1995, the UK was responsible for about 2.5 per cent of the world's carbon dioxide emissions, with emissions of just under 10 tonnes of carbon dioxide per capita (over twice the world average, **Figure 15**).[204]

By 2020, without additional policies, it is expected that the UK's share of world emissions will have fallen to about 1.4 per cent, but risen slightly in absolute terms to about 10 tonnes of carbon dioxide per capita (1.8 times the world average).[205] Current levels are about four tonnes per capita as a world average, with a maximum emission of over 20 tonnes per capita in the USA. To reduce Britain's per capita emissions to the global average would require them to be more than halved.

"The most promising, and just, basis for securing long term agreements is to allocate emissions rights to nations on a per capita basis – enshrining the idea that every human is entitled to release into the atmosphere the same quantity of greenhouse gases. But because of the very wide differences between per capita emission levels around the world, and because current global emissions are already above safe levels, there will have to be an adjustment period covering several decades in which nations' quotas converged on the same per capita level. This is the principle of contraction and convergence" Royal Commission on Environmental Pollution, 2000.[206]

Trade-related transportation has been estimated to account for one eighth of world oil consumption, which means that international air, sea and road freight transport are a significant source of greenhouse gases.

Although governments are now committed to reductions in domestic greenhouse gas emissions, the carbon dioxide emissions associated with the transport involved in international trade are not included in national reduction targets, agreed as part of the Kyoto Protocol. There is therefore no incentive to reduce emissions from international freight transportation by sea and air.

On a more personal level, the annual carbon dioxide (CO2) emissions associated with a 'typical' four-bedroom semi-detached house built to 1995 Building Regulation standards amount to 4.2 tonnes (**Table 9**). Another significant source of carbon dioxide emissions is personal travel. A medium sized petrol car averaging 20,000 kilometres a year will emit 4.4 tonnes of CO2. **However, it has been estimated that the CO2 emissions attributable to producing, processing, packaging and distributing the food consumed by a family of four is about 8 tonnes a year.**[207]

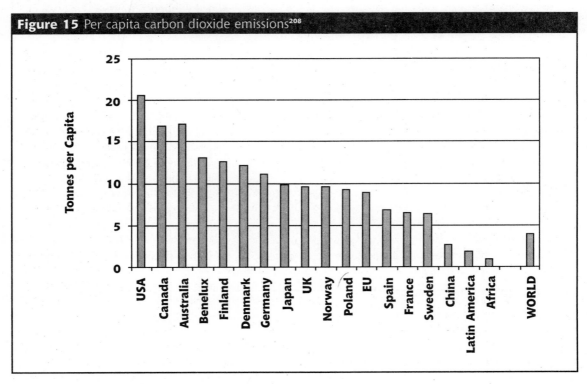

Figure 15 Per capita carbon dioxide emissions[208]

4.2.2 Climate change: The consequences

"Some climate change is now inevitable – the greenhouse gases that have already accumulated in the atmosphere mean that we cannot avoid some rise in temperature. But the worst effects of climate change can be avoided if the world acts now to reduce emissions and, in time, stabilise the levels of carbon dioxide in the atmosphere" [209]

Climate change is predicted to cause major adverse effects on the world's ecosystems, including more extreme weather events, rising sea levels affecting coastal and low lying areas, and loss of habitats and species. If we continue to burn fossil fuels at present rates, the concentration of greenhouse gases in the atmosphere will increase by 50 per cent within 15 years – risking catastrophic climate shifts.[210] Temperatures could rise by 2.3°C in the next 50 years and by 5.8°C by 2100, the most rapid increase in human history, which could result in a rise in sea levels of 15-95cm.[211] Unless urgent action is taken, temperatures at the Arctic could rise by 8°C. If we take a 'business as usual' approach to these threats the consequences could be devastating:

- Over the last 10 years, environmental disasters have caused over $600 billion worth of damage.[212] If current trends continue, by 2065 the economic costs of natural disasters could exceed world economic output.[213]
- The poorest countries are likely to be the most vulnerable to the effects of climate change and now face acute shortages of freshwater, slumps in food production, devastating floods and disastrous droughts. Of the additional 80 million people projected to be at risk of flooding, 60 per cent are expected to be in Southern Asia (Pakistan, India, Sri Lanka, Bangladesh and Myanmar (formerly Burma)) and 20 per cent in South East Asia (from Thailand to Vietnam, including Indonesia and the Philippines).[214]
- More than 290 million more people could be at risk of more serious strains of malaria. Malaria, spread by mosquitoes, could enter the UK and water supplies would be affected by toxic algal bloom.[215]
- There could be substantial 'die-back' of tropical forests and grasslands. By the 2070s, large parts of northern Brazil and central southern Africa could lose their tropical forests because of water shortage. If this happens, global vegetation, which currently absorbs carbon dioxide at the rate of some 2-3 gigatonnes of carbon (GtC) per year, will become a carbon source generating about 2 GtC per year by the 2070s and adding to further carbon dioxide build up in the atmosphere. (Current global emissions are about 6-7 GtC per year).[216]
- It has been suggested that warming could trigger the collapse of the West Antarctic Ice Sheet and result in a global sea level rise of five metres. It has also been suggested that the Gulf Stream could be affected, cooling the UK and the rest of north-western Europe. The probability of such events is considered to be low at the moment but they are hard to quantify and the risks need to be better understood in view of the importance of the Gulf Stream to the UK's climate and evidence of changes to its behaviour in the past.[217]

Increases in severe and unusual weather events such as floods and droughts could have a devastating effect on food production.

Countries in the South are expected to be hit the hardest. Africa is expected to experience significant reductions in cereal yields, as are the Middle East and India.[218] However, it is predicted that agriculture in Europe and North America will also be affected. Heavy rain and flooding in the UK in the autumn of 2000 led to reduced yields and crop losses. Damage to farm buildings and crop losses from flooding in the UK in that year have been estimated at half a billion pounds - much of it uninsurable.[219] It was predicted that the cost of grain could rise by £10 a tonne, leading to an increase of as much as 2p a loaf following one of the wettest years on record in 2000, with southern England suffering the heaviest downpours since 1727.[220] The 2001 wheat crop in the UK was a quarter less than the previous year.

In the UK, thousands of apple trees in the south-west could also be lost as a result of flooding in 2000. It is believed that the capillaries in the root system were in effect 'drowned', pushing out all oxygen. This was discovered 8 months after the flooding as the leaves turned black, a result of toxins being pushed upwards from the root system. In Southern Europe droughts are becoming more frequent. In Greece, rainfall in the seven months to March 2001 was 40 per cent below average in some regions, resulting in 20 per cent of the grain crop being lost. The Agriculture minister has stated that "this is a crisis year" and decided to run a trial 'artificial rain programme'.[221]

A recent United Nations Environment Programme (UNEP) report has presented evidence that rising temperatures, linked with emissions of greenhouse gases, can damage staple food crops such as wheat, rice and maize.[222] The findings, based on research at the Manila-based International Rice Research Institute (IRRI), estimate that harvests of some of the world's key food crops could drop by up to 30 percent in the next 100 years due to global warming. Yields could fall by as much as 10 per cent for every one degree Celsius rise in areas such as the Tropics. Key cash crops such as coffee and tea in some of the major growing regions will also be vulnerable over the coming decades to global warming.

The report quotes UNEP Executive Director Klaus Toepfer as saying that *"billions of people across the tropics depend on crops such as rice, maize and wheat, for their very survival…These new findings indicate that large numbers are facing acute hunger and malnutrition unless the world acts to reduce emissions of carbon dioxide and other greenhouse gases."* [223]

Clearly the evidence for climate change is there and there can be little doubt of the potentially disastrous impact on the environment and on communities worldwide. The contribution food production and trade makes is significant and on the increase.

4.3 Other polluting consequences of food miles

Increasing congestion, local air pollution and emissions of greenhouse gases are only a few of the direct effects of road transport. Additionally, noise and vibration, fumes and dirt, accidents, the land use of transport infrastructure and the destruction of wildlife habitats, are all 'external' costs of a road-based transport system. The impact of air emissions originating from road transportation is to be observed at every level from local to global. These range from localised effects (for example, the toxicity of carbon monoxide) through regional effects (such as ground-level ozone episodes) and national and transnational effects (acid deposition) to the global significance of carbon dioxide as a greenhouse gas contributing to what could be irreversible climate change.[224]

Air pollution problems vary according to the concentration of the pollutant, the duration of exposure of the affected population or environment and the toxicology of the pollutant. In some cases damage will not occur until a certain threshold level is exceeded, in others the effects will be felt immediately. Although this report focuses on carbon dioxide, being the main greenhouse gas, other emissions also have an environmental impact and affect human health. Diesel and petrol exhaust fumes are considered respectively to be 'probably' and 'possibly' cancer causing. Road vehicle emissions provide the bulk of most peoples exposure to numerous toxic substances. Over four hundred chemical compounds have been identified in exhaust emissions and fuel vapour from petrol and diesel vehicles, including organic hydrocarbons, 1,3-butadiene, benzene, formaldehyde and polyaromatic hydrocarbons, esters, ethers, nitriles and organometallic compounds, many of which are known or probable cancer causing substances.[225]

In a report in 1998, Government experts concluded that between 12,000 and 24,000 people might die prematurely every year as a result of short-term exposure to air pollution.[226] The report added that a further 14,000 to 24,000 hospital admissions and re-admissions may also be caused by exposure to air pollution. The incidence of asthma has more than doubled in the last 15 years with one in seven children now affected.[227] Evidence of a link between pollution and asthma is accumulating, even if there is no proof yet of a causal relationship. What is known, however, is that pollution can aggravate asthma symptoms and can also trigger an asthma attack in people who are already asthmatic.[228]

Within the UK, transport systems are responsible for 73, 47, 57 and 26 per cent of all carbon monoxide, nitrogen oxides, lead and particulate emissions, respectively.[229] The health and ecological effects of particulates, nitrogen dioxide, carbon monoxide, benzene and smog are as significant:[230][231]

Particulate matter: is a complex mixture of organic and inorganic substances in the atmosphere. Particulates can aggravate diseases like bronchitis and asthma by irritating the respiratory system, exacerbating morbidity and mortality from respiratory dysfunction. Diesel particulates are classified as probable carcinogens while suspended particulates have the ability to absorb carcinogens.

Nitrogen dioxide: causes altered/reduced lung function as well as lung tissue damage and the development of emphysema-like lesions in the lungs; acute respiratory illness and irritation of the respiratory tract; and increased susceptibility to viral infection. Nitrogen dioxide also plays a major role in acid deposition in Europe.

Carbon monoxide: is a toxic, colourless, odourless and tasteless gas that combines with haemoglobin in the blood thereby reducing the blood's oxygen-carrying capacity. Exposure to high concentrations results in loss of consciousness and death. At lower concentrations, it affects the functioning of the central nervous system.

Benzene: A known carcinogen which can cause leukemia.

Photochemical Smog: is a complex mixture of pollutants which can form in hot sunny weather. Ozone is one of the main components of photochemical smog. Chronic heart disease, asthma, bronchitis and emphysema can all be aggravated. Ozone causes headaches, coughing, damage to the lungs and reduces resistance to illness. Ozone also reduces vegetation growth and can therefore affect commercial crops.

Table 12 Air pollution resulting from freight transport[232]

	Journey	Distance (kilometres)	Emissions (grammes per tonne load)		
			Hydrocarbons	Nitrogen oxides	Carbon monoxide
Ship	Valencia to London	3150	126	1,260	378
	Auckland to London	22992	920	9,197	2,759
Truck	Madrid to London	1600	480	5,760	3,840
	Greece to London	3300	990	11,880	7,920
Air	California to London	8774	17,548	48,257	12,284
	Auckland to London	18839	37,678	103,614	26,375

Table 13 Air pollution resulting from shopping trips by car

	Distance* (kilometres)	Emissions (grammes)		
		Hydrocarbons	Nitrogen oxides	Carbon monoxide
Car (7 years old)[233]	8	3.4	2.6	50.6
	70	32.0	23.1	443.1
Car (typical 2001 model)[234]	8	0.9	0.8	5.3
	70	7.7	6.6	46.2

* see Box 3

Tables 12 and 13 show the pollution resulting from freight transport and shopping trips. For example, when foodstuffs are imported from New Zealand by plane this results in 103 kilograms of nitrogen oxide emissions per tonne and a shopping trip by car can produce 443 grammes of toxic carbon monoxide.

The movement of a tonne of goods from New Zealand by plane results in three and a half times more nitrogen oxide emissions than average annual per capita nitrogen oxide emissions within the UK and a third of UK per capita carbon monoxide emissions.

Environmental damage is not restricted to the effects of vehicle exhausts. Other sources of particulates, many of which are of respirable size, arise from tyre abrasion and braking systems including asbestos, chrome, nickel, copper, zinc, cadmium, cobalt and aluminium. Moreover, pollution occurs throughout the life cycle of a vehicle, beginning with the extraction of the raw materials required, through its useful life, to final disposal.

It has been estimated that the energy consumed during vehicle manufacture can amount to a quarter of the energy consumed in the life of the vehicle.[235]

Maintenance and spare-parts supply and disposal also have an environmental impact and further threats to the environment result from the resource and energy consumption associated with transport infrastructure. Demands for large areas of land for roads, car parks and service stations continue to destroy not only unique wildlife habitats and areas of outstanding natural beauty, but also parts of our towns, homes, historic sites, and recreational areas which add to the quality of life for many people.[236]

In terms of transport infrastructure, it is important to recognise the direct environmental impact at the location of the construction, at the source of the construction materials and the transportation of the materials to the construction site. For each kilometre of six lane motorway 100,000 tonnes of aggregate is required or approximately 5,000 lorry loads.[237] The extraction process for aggregates is itself energy-intensive and the sites for quarrying, especially in the South-East of England, are becoming scarce, which results in the transportation from quarries in Somerset, the north of England and the north-west of Scotland, as well as imports.

Road construction represents approximately 30 per cent of the total energy consumption in the life cycle of freight vehicles.[238]

It is important that consumers are aware of these effects on the environment and their health. The transport associated with food distribution should be of particular interest to organic consumers. One of the principles of the International Federation of Organic Agricultural Movements (IFOAM) for organic agriculture is to avoid all forms of pollution that may result from agricultural production.

By avoiding the use of synthetic pesticides and fertilisers, organic farming reduces pollution. However, the long distance transportation of organic food, particularly by plane, lorry and car, will result in significant pollutant emissions, many of which are as toxic as pesticides.

4.4 Accidents will happen: Seabirds eating oil

In many cases oil production has resulted in devastating ecological and human health effects. The tankers that distribute oil have regularly been involved in spills. For example, on Thursday 15th February 1996 the tanker *Sea Empress* ran aground at the entrance to Milford Haven. *Sea Empress* was a 147,000 tonnes single-hulled tanker, on passage from the Firth of Forth, Scotland, to the Texaco Refinery in Milford Haven. When she left the Firth of Forth she was laden with 131,000 tonnes of Forties Blend crude oil and about 2,400 tonnes of fuel oil.

Although three large salvage tugs were brought in, on the evening of Saturday 17th February they were not able to hold her against the combination of wind and strong tide and she was swept on to rocks, suffering further damage and releasing more oil. During the following three days more groundings occurred and more oil was released. The grounding of the *Sea Empress* released 72,000 tonnes of crude oil and about 360 tonnes of heavy fuel oil making this incident the third largest in UK coastal waters and among the 20 largest spills ever.[239] Allowing for evaporation there was the potential for 43,000 tonnes of oil to come ashore. Aerial spraying of dispersants and recovery of some oil at sea meant that about 3-5,000 tonnes of oil reached the shoreline, some 200 kilometres of which was affected. The largest spill, that of the Amoco Cadiz in Brittany in 1978 killed an estimated 25,000 birds.[240] Oil spills cause significant ecological damage and adversely affect marine life and sea birds.

4.5 Nutritional implications of long distance food

Some studies have reported that, since 1940, there has been a significant decline in trace elements in fruits and vegetables: calcium content is down by 46 per cent and copper by 75 per cent.[241] In terms of vegetable varieties, carrots have lost 75 per cent of their magnesium and broccoli has lost 75 per cent of its calcium. These trace metals have numerous health benefits and virtually all of our intake comes from fruits, vegetables and nuts.

Two possible explanations of these findings are: first that modern industrialised cultivation techniques, through the use of synthetic fertilisers have increased the basic nitrogen, phosphorus and potassium (NPK) growth elements at the expense of other factors; and second, plant breeding, which has concentrated on disease resistance, appearance and shelf life has neglected trace element content.

The nutritional content of foods has also been reduced due to a longer time period between harvesting and consumption as food supply chains have been extended. The terms "garden fresh" and "market fresh" are sometimes used to distinguish the difference in nutrient content in fruits and vegetables at the point of harvest (garden fresh) and when they arrive at the market (market fresh). In general, the shorter the time between the harvesting of fruits and vegetables and consumption, the higher the nutrient content.

As fresh produce is usually stored and transported to market, some nutrient losses will occur even with excellent storage conditions. Most often it is vitamin C and A that are lost, with the decrease in vitamin C content beginning immediately after harvesting (**Table 14**). Further loss of vitamin C occurs when the fruits or vegetables are bruised or the leaves wilt.[242] Vitamin A losses are due mainly to the length of time that the product is stored rather than storage temperature. To a lesser extent, riboflavin and vitamin E are also susceptible to losses during storage and transportation as these vitamins are sensitive to light, oxygen and heat (**Table 15**). Minerals are generally more stable than vitamins.

Table 14 Loss of vitamin C in leafy vegetables after harvest[243]

Time after harvest (hours)	Loss (%)
2	5 - 18
4	10 - 30
8	35 - 60
10	38 - 66
24	90

Table 15 Summary of factors which may reduce some nutrients in fresh produce[244]

Nutrient	Heat	Light	Air
Vitamin A	yes, with air	no	yes, with heat
Thiamin*	yes	no	yes
Riboflavin	no	yes	no
Folate	yes	no	yes, but protected by vitamin C
Vitamin C*	yes	yes	Yes

* Least stable to storage

Green beans for instance stored for only 24 hours at room temperature were found by one study to have lost 24 per cent of their vitamin C; this was reduced to 10 per cent at 10°C.[245] About 10 to 50 per cent of nutrients may be lost during the weeks that typically pass between harvesting and arriving on the supermarket shelf. A study carried out on fresh peas and spinach has also demonstrated that antioxidant activity in fresh vegetables tends to reduce over time.[246] Fresh apples, oranges, carrots and grapefruit are inclined to preserve their nutritive value longer. Others, including kale, broccoli and green beans may lose theirs quickly.

It is virtually impossible for consumers to determine the length of time from the field to the table for foods that they buy. Some fruits and vegetables are stored for long periods a coldstore in modified temperature and atmosphere conditions. Apples, for example, are often stored this way for between 3 and 12 months.[247] If the product is not kept in coldstore, the time between harvesting and retail outlet will be greatest when imported by ship. For example, a bulk carrier travelling at a maximum speed of 11 knots will take 48 days to travel between New Zealand and the UK.[248]

Food processing can also reduce the nutrient value of foods. For example, frozen spinach that has been stored for six months has 50 per cent less vitamin C and 67 per cent less thiamin than when prepared from fresh spinach leaves.[249] Riboflavin losses in cooked, frozen peas are twice as high as cooked; fresh and during canning, tomato juice can lose up to 65 per cent vitamin C, 17 per cent of the niacin and 40 per cent of the carotene found in freshly picked tomatoes (**Table 16**). Thiamin (Vitamin B1) helps release energy from food, niacin (Vitamin B3) is vital for obtaining energy from glucose, and riboflavin (Vitamin B2) helps transfer energy from one compound to another.[250]

For healthy diets, UK fruit and vegetable consumption needs to double from the current level of around three portions a day, to at least five portions. However, in meeting this target, the goal of optimising nutritional intake will be achieved only if distance between producer and consumer and the amount of processing is minimised by developing local food schemes.

Whilst the evidence is not by any means complete, it suggests that the longer the food chain, the more potential there is for nutrient losses.

Table 16 Nutrient losses during the canning of tomato juice[251]

Nutrients	Percentage lost
Vitamin C	10 - 65
Thiamin	0 - 27
Riboflavin	0 - 14
Niacin	0 - 17
Carotene	25 - 40

4.6 Monoculture: trading out diversity, variety and food security

Many native people have a vested interest in maintaining a wide variety of animals and plants in their locality in order to reduce reliance on just one source of food. But encroachment by western-style civilisation and its farming methods means that many of these varieties are fast disappearing along with their genetic diversity. This is increasing the threat of crop failures across the globe as a result of genetic uniformity in agriculture.

More than 700 breeds of farm animals have already become extinct and 1,335 or 32 per cent are classified as being at high risk of loss or under threat of extinction.[252] Since 1995, the number of mammalian breeds at risk of extinction has risen from 23 to 35 per cent. The situation facing bird breeds is even more serious with the proportion at risk of loss put at 63 per cent in 1999. The greatest threat to domestic animal diversity is the export of animals from Northern to Southern countries, which often leads to cross-breeding or even replacement of local breeds.[253] In the Philippines, where thousands of traditional rice varieties were once cultivated by small farmers, just two Green Revolution varieties accounted for 98 per cent of all rice production in the mid-1980s.[254] Similarly, in the United States, more than 7000 apple varieties were grown in the last century. Now, over 85 per cent of these (more than 6000) are extinct and just two apple varieties account for more than half the entire US crop.[255]

The Convention on Biological Diversity, which is managed by United Nations Environment Programme and which grew out of the Rio Earth Summit of 1992, makes specific reference to the need to protect the world's indigenous cultures and traditions. Article eight of the convention states the need: "...*subject to its national legislation, (to) respect, preserve, and maintain knowledge, innovations and practices of indigenous and local communities embodying traditional life styles relevant for the conservation and sustainable use of biological diversity....*". However, research commissioned by UNEP has found that many indigenous languages and cultures are already teetering on the brink of extinction in the face of globalisation. Its report cites four key reasons why conserving native cultures should be urgently addressed:[256]

- ■ Traditional economic systems have a relatively low impact on biological diversity because they tend to utilise a great diversity of species, harvesting small numbers of each of them. By comparison settlers and commercial harvesters target far fewer species and collect or breed them in vast numbers, changing the structure of ecosystems.

- ■ Indigenous peoples try to increase the biological diversity of the territories in which they live, as a strategy for increasing the variety of resources at their disposal and, in particular, reducing the risk associated with fluctuations in the abundance of individual species.

- ■ Indigenous people customarily leave a large 'margin of error' in their seasonal forecasts for the abundance of plants and animals. By underestimating the harvestable surplus of each target species, they minimise the risk of compromising their food supplies.

- ■ Since indigenous knowledge of ecosystems is learned and updated through direct observations on the land, removing the people from the land breaks the generation to generation cycle of empirical study. Maintaining the full richness and detail of traditional knowledge depends on continued use of the land as a classroom and laboratory.

Examples include the native farmers of the Andean mountains who developed terraces, canals and raised fields, known as waru-waru, at nearly 4,000 metres above sea level over 3,000 years ago. The system, while appearing primitive to western eyes, has allowed the native peoples there to produce crops like potatoes and quinoa in the face of floods, droughts and severe frosts. This farming system also helps the farmers cope with temperature extremes. Meanwhile the system maintains soil fertility. Organic matter, silt and algae build-up in the canals and is dug out as a fertiliser. The waru-waru system is not only sustainable and environmentally friendly but also leads to higher yields. Studies indicate that potato yields, grown in this traditional farming system, are about 10 tonnes a hectare versus the regional average of one to four tonnes.[257]

Another recent study has shown that small farmers using simple, low-cost techniques with local inputs can increase production dramatically. These farming practices are approaching 'sustainable agriculture' because they aim to reduce water use, regenerate soils by using manure, prevent erosion though shallow ploughing and minimise the use of agro-chemicals. The study found that for the 4.42 million small farmers practising 'sustainable agriculture' on 3.58 million hectares of land, average food production increased by about 73 per cent per household. For those that were growing important staple crops such as potatoes and cassava, the increase was about 150 per cent whilst larger farms in Latin America increased total production by 46 per cent.[258]

Although these traditional farming systems are environmentally efficient, they are not regarded as economically efficient by many development analysts. As a result they are under threat as the World Bank and International Monetary Fund have encouraged the adoption of high-input specialised farming.

4.7 Misery Miles

In 1998, 12.2 million pigs, cattle and sheep were transported between EU member states, including 6.8 million pigs, 2.9 million cattle and 2.5 million sheep. The main importers of live animals are Italy, Germany and Spain. In 1998, Italy imported 800,000 sheep, 1.5 million cattle and 1.1 million pigs.[259] The extent of these movements is shown in **Table 17**.

The UK exports just under one million sheep a year for slaughter, many being sent all the way to Italy and Greece, and the figures are rising.

Large quantities of meat and live animals are also imported into the EU from South America, Eastern Europe, and Africa. For example, in 1999 44,000 tons of live bovine animals and meat were imported from Argentina together with 11,000 tons from Botswana, 40,000 tons from Poland and over 70,000 tons from Brazil.[261] In this year the EU also exported 874,211 tons of live bovine animals and meat to the rest of the world.

This cruel trade to and fro in animals represents a huge welfare problem both in terms of the welfare of the animals in transit, and the quality of care where the animals arrive at the destination.

Table 17 Movements of live pigs in the EU, 1998 [260]

Recipient	Source TOTAL	France	Bel/Luk	Neths	Germany	Italy	UK	Ireland	Denmark	Greece	Portugal	Spain	Sweden	Finland	Austria
FRANCE	393,856		84,408	153,231	105,934	2,936	6,911	4,120	12	0	0	36,073	0	0	231
BEL/LUX	940,882	124,790		371,205	413,320	236	21,139	311	1,225	0	0	0	0	0	8,656
NETHS	174,655	19,493	79,357		63,917	1,762	6,093	650	2,370	0	0	0	0	0	1,013
GERMANY	2,505,366	767	88,275	1,010,491		0	28,820	5,643	1,336,099	0	0	405	3,031	0	31,835
ITALY	1,127,710	133,084	301,207	404,252	138,701		8,014	29,555	21,612	0	0	79,848	96	0	11,341
UK	203,174	0	0	64	0	0		198,230	4,880	0	0	0	0	0	0
IRELAND	9,470	0	0	0	0	0	9,470		0	0	0	0	0	0	0
DENMARK	712	0	0	0	0	0	0	0		0	0	0	712	0	0
GREECE	5,279	267	67	3,092	108	500	1,102	0	143		0	0	0	0	0
PORTUGAL	242,620	302	251	2,283	0	0	1,445	0	0	0		238,339	0	0	0
SPAIN	1,108,917	306,854	6,541	629,270	109,073	5,218	26,559	0	0	401	25,001		0	0	0
SWEDEN	0	0	0	0	0	0	0	0	0	0	0	0		0	0
FINLAND	0	0	0	0	0	0	0	0	0	0	0	0	0		0
AUSTRIA	164,421	582	8,905	2,090	152,794	0	0	0	7	0	0	0	0	43	
	6,877,062	586,139	569,011	2,575,978	983,847	10,652	109,553	238,509	1,366,348	401	25,001	354,665	3,839	43	53,076

4.8 Importing disease and microbial miles

Britain in 2001 experienced a silent spring. The countryside was effectively closed to the public and in many areas there were no farm animals to be seen. The cause was an outbreak of Foot and Mouth Disease (FMD), the first case of which was confirmed on February 20th. The relentless spread of the disease was a blow for farmers and the tourist industry, whose losses climbed to millions of pounds each week. There were also concerns about animal welfare, as animals were slaughtered in large numbers on farms, and also about the effects on human health of dioxin emissions from the burning pyres. In County Durham almost 900 cattle and sheep had to be exhumed following fears that the carcasses would pollute a underground spring between two villages.

The previous outbreak in the UK had been in 1967, when almost all cases were confined to Shropshire, Staffordshire and Cheshire, with a few occurring in adjoining counties. The present outbreak spread more extensively and more rapidly partly because of intensive livestock production and finishing methods and unnecessary movements of live animals within the UK. Increasingly animals are kept in cramped conditions and fed with antibiotics to fend off diseases.[262] When the animals leave the farm they are routinely transported hundreds of miles before slaughter. This time, within the first week, the 12 confirmed cases were located as far apart as Northumberland, Devon and Essex. After only three weeks FMD had spread to many regions of the UK, south of the Firth of Forth. By April 4th the number of cases had risen to 1000 and reached 1,880 on 23 July, by which time more than three and a half million animals had been slaughtered. Between May and August, the number of new confirmed cases remained at between 1 and 8 each day.

Animals are now transported longer distances because of changes in livestock distribution and meat processing systems in the UK and increases in international trade (See **Box 5**). Almost two-thirds of UK abattoirs have closed down in the last 10 years.[263] One reason for these closures is increased inspection costs since BSE, another is the demise of independent butchers and the emergence of centralised systems operated by the multiple retailers. Investigating the latest outbreak, MAFF (now DEFRA) found that pigs had been sent for slaughter to the Cheale Meats abattoir in Essex, where FMD was first identified, from more than 600 farms, as far away as Scotland and Northern Ireland.[264] This is a result of centralisation in livestock systems (for example, one abattoir now slaughters 60 per cent of the UK's cull sows) and a growing trade in animal dealing, both of which result in long-distance transportation of live animals. One of the sheep farms in Devon that was affected early on by foot and mouth was exporting live sheep to the continent.[265] Movements of this type risk transmitting disease across Europe.

"Some [lambs] get moved from one fatstock market to the next, first to get, hopefully, an increase in price...Some sheep which landed up in France actually came from Worcestershire and had gone to three markets before arriving in Longtown, then been shipped to Northern Ireland, down through the border to Southern Ireland and then exported to France as Irish lambs... Animal welfare implications must be horrendous for the lambs... These poor creatures were probably loaded six times before they went to the abattoir" Francis Anthony, former president of the British Veterinary Association.[266]

One question that has to be asked about the Foot and Mouth crisis is why a disease that does no permanent harm to humans and from which most animals recover in a matter of weeks, has virtually shut down the countryside, downgraded vaccination in favour of massive slaughter of healthy animals, and crippled the UK tourist industry? Many believe this has occurred purely to ensure that we can continue to export meat.

The UK earns £630 million per year from meat and dairy exports. One estimate of the cost of the Foot and Mouth epidemic in terms of losses predominantly to tourism, but also to farming, was put at £9 billion. If this is the total cost of FMD, that means that it will take more than 14 years of exports to compensate for the damage done in the 'cull to eradicate' approach to Foot and Mouth.[267]

There are seven separate virus types that cause FMD. The strain recently discovered in the UK is called serotype O of the pan-Asian strain. It was first identified in India in 1990 and spread westwards into Saudi Arabia in 1994 and, subsequently, throughout the near East and into Europe. In 1993 it was found in Nepal and later in Bangladesh and Bhutan. In 1999 it had reached Southeast Asia and entered South Africa in 2000. The FAO believes FMD remains a serious risk as a result of increased international trade, tourism, the movement of animals, animal products and foodstuffs.[268]

Peter Roeder of the FAO believes that Central Asia is a back door into Europe if diseases spread via Russia and Eastern Europe.[269] Other pig diseases such as Post-weaning Multisystemic Wasting Syndrome (PMWS) and Porcine Dermatitis and Nephropathy Syndrome (PDNS) have become endemic across the UK. While the livestock industry was still reeling from FMD and BSE in August 2001, thousands of UK pig farms were infected by PMWS, an untreatable condition that increases piglet mortality more than threefold and is thought to be present in up to two-thirds of the industry. PMWS was first identified in Canada in 1991 and arrived in Britain in 1998.[270] Three major endemic and highly contagious diseases currently pose serious threats to Pakistan, Afghanistan and the Central Asia republics: FMD, rinderpest and *Peste des petits ruminants*.

The Foot and Mouth outbreak indicates that imported food needs careful policing to guarantee its safety. This is a daunting and ever growing task. At Felixstowe where half our containerised food imports enter the country it is up to the small team of nineteen inspectors from the port health authority to spot-check tens of thousands of containers arriving directly from all over the world. Under EU regulations food is inspected at its port of entry into Europe, which means that any container inspected elsewhere in the Union will not be inspected here. Recent seizures by Suffolk Coastal officers include ham from China and pork jerky and dried milk products from outside the EU. As well as the spread of an animal virus such as Foot and Mouth, the consumption of these products could also make people ill.

Legal imports are also of concern as pests imported on fruit, vegetables, grain and timber could lead to infestation. For example, a colony of Colorado Beetles, which can devastate potato crops, was discovered in the UK in 1977 and in 1992 about 500 were found in a consignment of imported lettuce. Although the species is not currently established in the UK, a single female beetle could form a breeding colony. A report from MAFF (now DEFRA), *Climate Change and Agriculture in the UK*, concluded that the area of the UK in which the beetle could survive would double with an increase in temperature of 1.8°C. The UK is expected to see more pests in the future because of global warming.[271]

Box 5 The sourcing and distribution of livestock and meat products.

Australian Beef[272]

One study has found that it is possible for an Australian beef animal and the subsequent products to pass through 24 stages before reaching the UK consumer (see below). The cumulative distance the product is transported is likely to be considerably greater than the shipping distance of 20,000 kilometres. In a chain of this length "The chain is often very secretive about the price dynamics of its operations... there is the possibility for considerable poor communication, distrust and power manipulation." In reality meat from one animal may go to a number of markets. For example, it has been estimated that an American hamburger may contain the meat from 20-120 different animals.[273]

Beef from Australia to the UK consumer

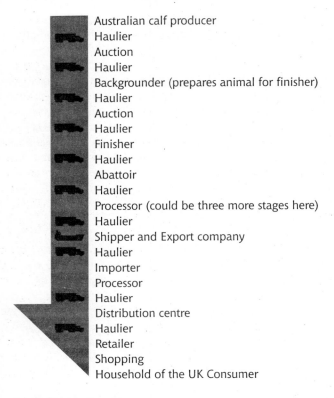

Australian calf producer
Haulier
Auction
Haulier
Backgrounder (prepares animal for finisher)
Haulier
Auction
Haulier
Finisher
Haulier
Abattoir
Haulier
Processor (could be three more stages here)
Haulier
Shipper and Export company
Haulier
Importer
Processor
Haulier
Distribution centre
Haulier
Retailer
Shopping
Household of the UK Consumer

New Zealand Lamb[274]

Fielding Lamb Packers (FLP) and Advanced Foods New Zealand (AFNZ) form part of another example of a highly centralised supply chain that is based on the principle of DIFONTTSAAP or Delivery In Full ON Time To Specification At Agreed Price. FLP is one of three abattoirs that work together and are known as The Progressive Group. They supply lamb carcasses to AFNZ via a single cutting and boning plant. AFNZ are in turn partners with Bernard Mathews UK who manage the New Zealand lamb category for Tesco. To work on achieving high specifications the chain is currently examining the genetic base of the system to look at breeding specific strains for specific market requirements. The system suits larger farmers better and there has also been a concentration in the New Zealand slaughter and processing sector, as there has been in the dairy sector. It is possible that in a few years time three firms will control the all red meat output in New Zealand. New Zealand also has formal alliances with at least nine other countries with a view to supplying contracts for chilled lamb 365 days a year. This has even resulted in the relocation of a New Zealand abattoir to China. Such a global perspective - how can we fulfil contracts and where in the world can we go to do it most profitably - is increasingly dominating the global food industry. The official line is that New Zealand lamb is a complimentary product to UK lamb. The industry perspective is slightly different as it would like to supply as much of the product as possible 365 days of the year.

Local Welsh Beef

One television programme has traced the route by which supposedly local beef reaches a supermarket store in Tonypandy in South Wales.[275] The cattle are reared in Kidwelly but are transported 140 miles to Caernarfon in North Wales for slaughter and then back to Crosshands in South Wales for processing and packaging. The next stage is 125 miles by lorry to the regional distribution centre (RDC) of the multiple retailer in Tewkesbury, from where the beef is driven 90 miles to the supermarket in Tonypandy. The four transport stages involved in getting the product there involve a journey of 500 miles, 10 times the direct distance from the farm to the store. The meat processing plant at Crosshands supplies RDCs across Britain as far away as Scotland, which means that the beef miles in many instances will be significantly greater than 500 miles.

4.9 Food trade – help or hindrance to development?

"The WTO Agreement on Agriculture (AOA) brought agriculture into GATT for the first time... The AOA was opposed by many Southern governments as being biased to the advantage of Northern interests and they only agreed to it under pressure from the US and Europe... The free trade vision of the WTO AOA is a disaster for the food security of poor countries, as subsistence farms are increasingly replaced by export production" Colin Hines.[276]

Food production for export has been put forward as a model for agriculture in poorer, less industrialised countries (largely in the Southern hemisphere). Against a backdrop of continued international inaction on poverty alleviation and debt reduction for poor countries, such a position is understandable. However, there are concerns that this often involves specialised and high external-input production of a few relatively low-value cash crops for which world prices have fluctuated significantly in recent decades. Prices for primary commodities (excluding oil) have fallen by 50 per cent over the past 20 years, and the trend is set to continue.[277]

For countries that have become dependent on exporting these commodities, globalisation is directly responsible for their economic decline. The loans which have allowed these countries to 'develop' in this way are provided by the International Monetary Fund (IMF) and the World Bank. In order to qualify for the loans governments are required to carry out drastic economic reforms in what are referred to as structural adjustment programmes (SAPs). A significant component of SAPs is maximising foreign earnings which encourages an export-oriented economy together with free and open markets for foreign imports.[278] To obtain export earnings, IMF and World Bank policies have encouraged more and more farmers in Southern countries to move away from food production for local consumption to become dependent on a just a few 'cash crops' such as coffee, tea, cocoa and, more recently, horticultural products. The result has been over-supply and the values of many food commodities has plummeted.

A recent United Nations report on the world's 48 poorest countries has shown that although these countries have gone further than most in opening up their economies, they have been driven deeper into poverty.[279] Another report, which looked at the experience of 16 countries from the South following the implementation of the Uruguay Round Agreement on agriculture, found that the Agreement led to a surge in food imports but not exports.[280] The study, by the Food and Agriculture Organisation (FAO) showed that this is forcing local farmers out of business, resulting in displacement to urban areas and is leading to a concentration in farming.[281]

Some producers have found a niche market in Europe for the year-round supply of fruit, vegetables, and cut flowers. The UK is the largest market for Kenyan horticultural exports. However, this 'success' has a price. In an evaluation of fresh produce production for export, one study found that UK supermarkets, whilst having no investment there, control horticultural production in Kenya.[282] The large retailers deal predominantly with a small number of large-scale farms using high external-input and monocultural techniques, the same as they do in the UK.

Just three producers account for 45 per cent of Kenya's horticultural exports. By contrast, horticultural produce from Kenya destined for wholesale markets in the UK tends to be supplied by small and medium-sized growers and there is far more loyalty than in the case of supermarkets.[283]

In the 1990s the Kenyan horticultural industry underwent dramatic change with the 10 largest producers making huge investments in EU standard packhouses, refrigerated trucks and coldstores in order to attract and maintain contracts with UK multiple retailers. Kenyan producers proudly claim that, within 48 hours of being harvested, produce can be on the UK supermarket shelf. This can only be achieved if the produce is exported by plane and as a result 93 per cent of Kenya's fresh horticultural exports are air-freighted in cargo planes.[284]

The research also showed that horticultural products are cultivated in Kenya using large-scale and industrialised cultivation techniques rather than extensive and ecologically sustainable methods and concluded that retailer requirements in the UK encourage this.[285] Food trade liberalisation, together with the growing dominance of the multiple retailers has resulted in a relocation of unsustainable production to poorer countries to feed richer consumers.[286] This increased horticultural production and trade in Kenya has not even had the benefit one might expect; increased consumption of fruit and vegetables by Kenyans.

In 1979, Kenya produced 465,000 tonnes of vegetables and exported 5 per cent of this output (24,000 tonnes). By 1999 vegetable production had increased to 663,000 tonnes, and 9 per cent of this was exported (61,000 tonnes)[287] However, over this period, in which there was a 2.5-fold increase in exports, per capita vegetable consumption in Kenya decreased substantially from 25.1 to 18.1 kilograms per person per year (a 39 per cent reduction).

Over the same period Kenyan fruit exports almost doubled from 68,000 tonnes to 121,000 tonnes and again domestic consumption declined from 30.5 to 26.5 kilograms of fruit per person per year. In 1999 the world average consumption of vegetables and fruit was 97.2 and 59.7 kilograms per person per year, respectively. This means that in that year Kenyan vegetable consumption was only a fifth of, and fruit consumption was less than half, the world average.

The competitiveness of African suppliers of high-value horticultural produce depends on their low costs of production, complimentarity to European seasons, relatively short flight times and the ability to supply produce of the quality and quantity demanded by international markets. Although Kenya was one of the first African countries to move to horticultural production for export, and replaced Egypt as the main supplier of green beans to the EU, other countries are now competing for lucrative western markets. In a survey of horticultural producers, one claimed that The Gambia had taken Kenya's chilli market and others expressed concerns about competition from Zimbabwe, South Africa and West Africa.[288]

Supermarkets are in a powerful position to influence what is grown in Africa, how it is grown and by whom.[289] This also means uncertainty for horticultural enterprises, exporters and workers, as the retailers only accept delivery of produce and pay for it when it arrives in the UK and has been inspected. Competition between horticultural producers within Kenya as well as those in other African countries, together with more entrants into the market each year, compounds this uncertainty and means that they are in a similar situation to the producers of the more traditional cash crops (**See cocoa and banana examples below**).

Thailand has also embraced agricultural production for export in recent decades. **Table 18** shows that almost all of the increased production in rice, cassava, vegetables, fruit and meat in Thailand between 1979 and 1999 is exported. As a result, per capita intake of rice, fruit and vegetables has declined by over a quarter over this period.

Table 18 Thai food production, exports and consumption, 1979-1999[290]

	Production 1000 tonnes			Exports 1000 tonnes			Consumption Kg/capita/year		
	1979	1999	Change (%)	1979	1999	Change (%)	1979	1999	Change (%)
Cassava	11101	16507	49%	10816	14401	33%	8.9	11.0	24%
Meat	924	1861	101%	15	318	2020%	20.0	24.6	23%
Fruit	6293	7610	21%	230	1412	514%	123.0	91.1	-26%
Vegetables	2532	2774	10%	33	368	1015%	50.4	35.4	-30%
Rice	10511	15550	48%	2864	6977	144%	145.8	100.8	-31%

There have also been accusations that countries in which farming is subsidised, including the EU member states, have 'dumped' products on the South, which creates further problems. In 1994 Mexico opened its markets to competition from US agriculture following the introduction of the North American Free Trade Agreement (NAFTA). Within three years 800,000 Mexican farmers faced bankruptcy as a result of direct competition from industrial food production in the US.[291] Cattle farmers from Burkina Faso to South Africa have also been forced out of business due to cheap and heavily subsidised meat imports from the EU being dumped on African markets.[292]

Many more farmers have seen their livelihoods threatened when entering global markets. Coffee grown without fair trade protection is a good example of this threat. The world coffee price is largely dependent on production in Brazil, which produces around a quarter of the world's supply. When frost hit the Brazilian crop in 1994, the world coffee price rose. Variations in the Brazilian climate and economy are outside the control of coffee producers in Africa. Yet their integration into the global market means they have become vulnerable to such events. As the world market price of coffee is now in decline, African farmers who have been encouraged to convert from subsistence farming to coffee are increasingly unable to feed their families. As the World Development Movement has noted: *"Many have had to abandon farming and look for casual work in cities instead"*.[293]

Governments and the WTO have also favoured multinational companies over the smallholder farmers of the South. Within a day of the US Democratic Party receiving a $500,000 donation from banana multinational Chiquita, the Clinton government filed a complaint at the WTO against European trade agreements which favour bananas imported from small farmers in the Caribbean. The WTO's disputes settlement body ruled in favour of the US, demanding that it should have greater access to the lucrative European market. Up to 200,000 Caribbean farmers, many of them women, may lose their livelihoods as a result of the ruling.[294]

There is clearly a complex relationship between food supply and trade and the food security status of those in most need around the world. There is a requirement for appropriate food aid and emergency supplies in times of crises. However, during the famine in the 1980s, Ethiopia was a net exporter of grain and nearly 80 per cent of malnourished children in the South live in countries that have food surpluses.[295] The main threats to food security are: the inability of individuals, households and communities to meet their own food needs; climate change; and a dependency on erratic food export and import markets. Where hunger exists, what is often lacking is not food, but access to it – either having the money to buy it or the land to grow it on.[296] This applies in both Northern and Southern countries.[297] The potential of fairer trading relations as one way of tackling these issues is explored in more detail in the case studies below.

Many foods that have become everyday items in the shopping basket of UK consumers originate and can only be grown in the tropical regions of the world. Cocoa and bananas – fourth and fifth on the 'most important agricultural commodities in world trade' list - are typical examples.[298] The food miles travelled by such commodities are inevitably substantial. However, the largest leg of their journey – from country of origin to the UK - is usually made by ship, the most energy efficient form of bulk transportation. Richer consumers have come to expect ample year round supplies of these two commodities, whilst entire economies in the South have grown dependent on them for their survival.

Unfortunately, the environmental and socio-economic damage to Southern countries of conventional production of these commodities (particularly when this production takes place in large-scale intensive plantations) is often severe. Certified organic and fair trade production and supply systems are beginning to emerge as possible alternatives.

The fair trade movement emerged due to a growing awareness in industrialised nations that international trade is often unfair to producers. This is especially true for small scale farmers and rural workers in poorer countries. The two main aims of fair trade are to pay producers a decent price and to provide them with stable markets for their produce. Trade was seen as a longer-term and more self-reliant solution than aid. Originally applied to imports of craft products from Asia, Latin America and Africa, by the 1980s the idea had spread to food products.[299] The market for fair trade goods is those consumers able and willing to pay more in the knowledge that their economic exchange is fairer to the producer, and has continued to expand during the 1990s to include, among others, fair trade chocolate and bananas.

Case Study 1: Cocoa

The UK consumes considerable quantities of cocoa products. On average each British consumer spends £62.64 on chocolate a year - £1.20 per person every week. This amounts to approximately 15 per cent of the total British consumer expenditure on all foods.[300] In 1999, the UK imported 240,000 tonnes of cocoa beans. Nearly 90 per cent was from West Africa, with 38 per cent from Ghana, 33 per cent from Nigeria and 15 per cent from Ivory Coast. The largest supplier outside Africa is Indonesia, which produced 3.2 per cent of UK cocoa in 1997/98.[301] An estimated 70 per cent of world cocoa is grown by smallholders, largely in low input, low intensity agricultural systems.[302] In Ghana, for example, plantations account for only 1 per cent of cocoa production: most Ghanaian cocoa is grown on small family farms, usually inter-cropped with other plants and trees such as plantains, maize and spices. These provide shade as well as up to 65 per cent of the family's food supply, and additional income. Low world cocoa prices make yield losses due to pests a critical issue for farmers. However, very few can meet the rising costs of cocoa pesticides and spraying machines from the falling prices they receive for their cocoa. The Cocoa Research Institute of Ghana (CRIG) reports that almost half the farms in Ghana and one third in the Ivory Coast cannot afford to spray at all and are therefore 'organic by default', but do not receive a premium for this.[303 304]

Research from Ghana suggests that good husbandry, integrated pest management and minimal use of pesticides lead to yields similar to those obtained on intensive, high chemical input dependent plantations run by big multinational companies in countries such as Brazil.[305]

Despite this, Ghana is under pressure from manufacturers and the World Bank to go the way of Brazil and Malaysia with intensive estate-based production.[306] Much of this pressure stems from the current glut in world cocoa production which has led to an all time low in world prices, despite the fact that increased output from new plantations would only worsen the price problem. Moreover, a move away from a less intensive smallholder system to plantation cultivation frequently leads to rapid deterioration of social and environmental conditions. In plantations, cocoa trees are not grown in the shade for which they are adapted, and therefore need far more pesticides and other external inputs to produce high yields. This means increased energy consumption, water and soil pollution, loss of topsoil and fertility, loss of biodiversity, health hazards to plantation workers regularly exposed to pesticides - both whilst working and in their water supplies - and residues in the chocolate eaten by UK consumers.

Most of the estimated 27 million men, women and children enslaved around the world work in agriculture.[307] The media coverage of the 'Child Slave Ship' off the coast of Benin in West Africa in the Summer of 2001 brought international attention to the trafficking of children for agricultural labour in cocoa plantations. The United Nations Children's Fund (UNICEF) estimates more than 15,000 children from Mali are working in exploitative conditions in plantations in the Ivory Coast. They work more than 12 hours a day, seven days a week and earn a monthly 'salary' of about £10 a week, that is often not paid.[308] Supply chains are often so long and complex that a blind eye can easily be turned to the working conditions where the products originate. However, Save the Children believes that companies can no longer claim ignorance or a lack of responsibility for the conditions under which their goods are produced.[309]

One alternative approach is fairer trade obtained through farmers' and growers co-operatives. In Southern Ghana a group of Ghanaian farmers from several villages formed their own company, Kuapa Kokoo, to buy their cocoa and sell it direct to the Ghanaian Government Cocoa Buying Board. The Twin Trading fair trade company (makers of Cafedirect) supported Kuapa Kokoo, and The Day Chocolate Company, makers of fair trade chocolate, now buy their cocoa beans from the co-operative. These growers have obtained a better deal through bypassing some of the middlemen as well as by gaining direct and supportive links with the UK fair trade export market. This enables them to maintain and prosper on their own smallholdings which helps preserve environmental quality.[310]

Case Study 2: Bananas

Most of the 86 million tonnes of bananas and plantains produced annually are grown using few or no external inputs by millions of small-scale farmers in Africa, South Asia and Latin America for household consumption and/or local markets. Bananas consumed in the UK have traditionally come from the Windward Islands of the Caribbean where most production is in the hands of small farmers and the terrain is mountainous, making substantial economies of scale unfeasible. Farms are generally smaller than 5 hectares and are worked by numerous family members. They require less inputs than the large plantations of Latin America.[311]

Only 14 per cent of annual world production is traded on the world market, yet this 14 per cent is worth billions to the few multinational corporations who control it. Of the profits generated, workers on medium- and large-scale plantations and small farmers supplying the world market get only 1-3 per cent and 7-10 per cent respectively, and only 12 per cent of banana trade revenues remain in producing countries.

Once a producer grows for export, considerable and growing levels of external inputs are required to compete effectively. Plantations in Latin America are large and require road infrastructure, extremely sophisticated irrigation and drainage systems and cableway for harvesting. The plantations have pumping stations and one or more packing stations. Such facilities require enormous investment. Costs are kept low through low wages, limited workers' rights and precarious job tenure.[312] At the same time greater quantities of pesticides are used to improve yields in the face of escalating numbers of diseases affecting the banana plant.[313]

Banana production destined for export depends on chemical control. In Costa Rica alone, at least 280 different pesticides are authorised for use in banana cultivation. The financial cost of pesticides is huge - in some cases as much as 30-40 per cent of total costs. According to the International Union for the Conservation of Nature in 1995, the average use of pesticide in the banana plantations of Costa Rica was 44kg/ha/year - compared to an average 2.7 kg/ha/year for crops in industrialised countries. The EARTH College in Costa Rica estimates that of the fungicides applied by aeroplanes some forty times during each cultivation cycle, 15 per cent is lost to wind drift and falls outside the plantation, 40 per cent ends up on the soil rather than on the plants and approximately 35 per cent is washed off by rain. This results in a 90 per cent loss of the estimated 11 million litres of fungicide, water and oil emulsion applied each year in banana producing regions.[310]

Work in the banana plantations of Central America often consists of a 12 – 14 hour day, six days a week in tough conditions. Recently, following a protest over working conditions in one Costa Rican plantation owned by Costa Rica's ambassador to the UK, employees were sacked for being members of SITRAP, the banana plantation workers' union.[315] Announcing the sackings, the farm manager threatened the union workers that they would never be able to work on any banana plantation, adding that he hoped they would die from hunger.[316] As the union members met, a large container lorry left the nearby packing house with the Del Monte slogan – 'Say yes to the best'. Conditions have worsened for workers and national producers because of a 'banana crisis' caused by surpluses and a drop in prices as a result of the expansion of production in Costa Rica in the 1990s and, more recently, in Ecuador.[317]

Today almost 25,000 tonnes of bananas a year are produced and sold under fairer terms of trade: a ten-fold increase since 1995.[318] Fair trade has become essential in the struggle for survival of the banana growers in the Windward Islands of the Caribbean. As mentioned above, a World Trade Organisation ruling has overturned the longstanding protected status of these islands in supplying their bananas to Europe. This has exposed them to competition from Latin America, forcing around two thirds of Windward island banana growers who were supplying bananas to the UK market in 1993 to go out of business by 2000.[319] The 'Fairtrade Mark' is the label under which fair trade bananas are marketed in the UK. The Fairtrade price is based on the costs of production, processing and packaging in the country of origin plus an additional premium to enable growers' groups to invest in their future.[320]

4.10 Crude oil, food and human rights

In November 1995 Ken Saro-Wiwa and eight other Ogoni were executed in Nigeria for speaking out against the environmental damage to the Niger Delta caused by Shell Oil through its 37 years of drilling in the region. Ken Saro-Wiwa was campaigning for the most basic of human rights: the right for clean air, land and water.[321] For his work, Saro-Wiwa was nominated for the Nobel Peace Prize, and received the Goldman Environmental Prize.[322] The execution of Ken Saro-Wiwa in Nigeria focused attention on the collusion between multinationals and repressive regimes. Subsequent cases have included BP's operations in Columbia, where the British oil giant was accused of complicity in the murders of local protesters by paramilitary forces, Freeport's mining activities in Indonesia and Premier Oil in Burma.[323][324] A global report by Oxfam has shown that in oil and mineral exporting countries poverty has not been eliminated.[325] Indeed, the conclusion was that a dependency on resource exports exacerbates poverty by inducing forms of economic development that offer few direct benefits to the poor. In these countries there is a significant correlation between oil export dependence and corruption, authoritarian government and high levels of military spending, a heightened risk of civil war, poor healthcare and high rates of child mortality. Mineral rich countries were also found to be exceptionally vulnerable to economic shocks.

Following the Presidential elections in the USA, George W Bush has posed a new threat to indigenous people in Alaska. President Bush is heavily involved with the oil industry and has promised companies such as BP (which has donated hundred of thousand of dollars to the Republican Party) a free hand in drilling for oil in the protected Arctic National Wildlife Refuge.[326]

Nigeria, which is the largest oil producer in Africa, has been dependent on oil production and exports for several decades. This has been entrusted to the multinational oil conglomerates that have had the financial and technological means to invest in this sector.[327] Oil has, for the past three decades, provided 90-95 per cent of export revenues, 90 per cent of the foreign exchange earnings, and 80 per cent of total Nigerian government revenue.[328] Despite this significant income from oil exports, the 1980s and 1990s have been a time of agrarian stagnation and crisis in Nigeria. Food price inflation, the rapid increase in food imports and massive external debts are a few of the many problems related to the Nigerian military government's growth strategy.[329]

In Nigeria, pollution arising from careless and unmonitored oil production has resulted in severe strains on agriculture, fisheries, and human health.[330] The by-product of gas flaring continues to destroy the ecosystems of surrounding areas, and pipelines that have been constructed through numerous farmlands have ruptured, causing damage to vast areas of agricultural land.[331] Agriculture and fishing are a primary source of subsistence for a large portion of the Nigerian population, making up about 40 per cent of the nation's labour force.[332] The ecological damage caused by oil production therefore translates into depressed income, poor health and widespread poverty.

An additional shock to rural communities has been the displacement that has occurred over the course of oil exploration and production. It is estimated that 10,000 families from each of the six major oil producing regions have lost their farmlands to claims on areas for oil production and transportation alone, while further displacement results from oil pollution.[333] Important food crops such as cassava, pepper, garri, and cocoyam have all been subject to poor yields over the past few decades.[334] Other crops such as yellow yam, one of the most commonly grown species of yam in many communities, have disappeared from local markets. Apart from the loss of agricultural land as a result of oil production and pollution, agricultural policies, such as the conversion to cash crops and the introduction of other agricultural goods during the Green Revolution, have contributed to the scarcity of some of these foods. Between 1989 and 1995 the price of one foodstuff, a 25 kilogram bag of garri, increased by over 700 per cent and price of fish, a main source of protein for many tribes, has also risen, sometimes at a rate of 300 per cent a year.[335]

These problems are not restricted to Nigeria. Despite years of criticism of its environmental record, the World Bank continues to support projects in the South with potentially devastating environmental effects. In June 2000, for example, it approved a $365 million programme for the much criticised Chad-Cameroon oil pipeline, which will cut through the tropical rainforest of Cameroon and threaten farmland and river systems in both countries.[336]

5) A solution: Sustainable food supply chains

Sections three and four have described the dangers inherent in a food system that is based largely on minimising production costs in order to compete internationally. Maximising economic efficiency has led to economies of scale in food production and retailing and, as a result, sourcing decisions are now based mainly on securing large quantities of food products from wherever they can be produced at minimum financial cost. As a result, the environmental efficiency of food supply has declined in recent decades. Fossil fuel consumption, and resulting greenhouse gas emissions associated with the production, packaging and distribution of food has increased substantially. A sustainable food system is one in which fossil fuel consumption and, therefore, international trade in food is minimised.

5.1 Linear and circular food supply chains

Food supply chains (FSCs) comprise all the stages involved when delivering a food product to the consumer, including the subsequent waste management processes. For an individual fresh food product, for example, the FSC will involve one or more of the following: cultivation; sorting, processing and packaging; retailing; storage, preparation and consumption; and waste management, as well as the transport which link these activities, as they are often geographically dispersed. **Figure 16** illustrates FSCs in their most simplified form. FSCs will often be much more complicated: as described earlier, the production and supply of packaging as well as agricultural inputs involves numerous transport and process stages. A key indicator of environmental sustainability is the energy and material use associated with products.[337]

The main distinction between the contemporary food system and environmentally sustainable food supply chains is the 'linearity' or 'circularity' of the systems of production, distribution and waste management. Sustainable food supply chains minimise the throughput of energy and matter, by establishing a circular system.

5.1.1 Linear Food chains

Modern food production, packaging, distribution and waste management systems typically take a linear approach to energy and material throughput, which assume that at one end of the system there is an unlimited supply of energy and raw materials, while at the other the environment has an infinite capacity to absorb pollution and waste (**Figure 16**). The inevitable result, as soon as throughput is sufficiently increased, is resource shortages on the one hand and solid waste and air pollution problems on the other.[338] Although the global food system is complicated, and there are often many stages between farm and the consumer, it is not hard to see how this linear approach leads to problems. Even for fresh food products, such as fruit and vegetables, supply chains comprise numerous transport stages.

Each transport stage in the supply chain consumes derivatives of crude oil which results in air pollution. The movement of food products from the farm to the consumer often requires packaging in various forms and refrigeration, particularly when transported over long distances, and as the tomato sauce example in **Section 3.3** showed, it is not only food that is globally sourced but also packaging materials. When foodstuffs are processed there will be even more stages and more food miles. As discussed in section three, food miles cover not only the movement of food products and their packaging, but also the production and transportation of agricultural inputs.

Figure 16 Linear systems of food production, distribution and waste management.[339]

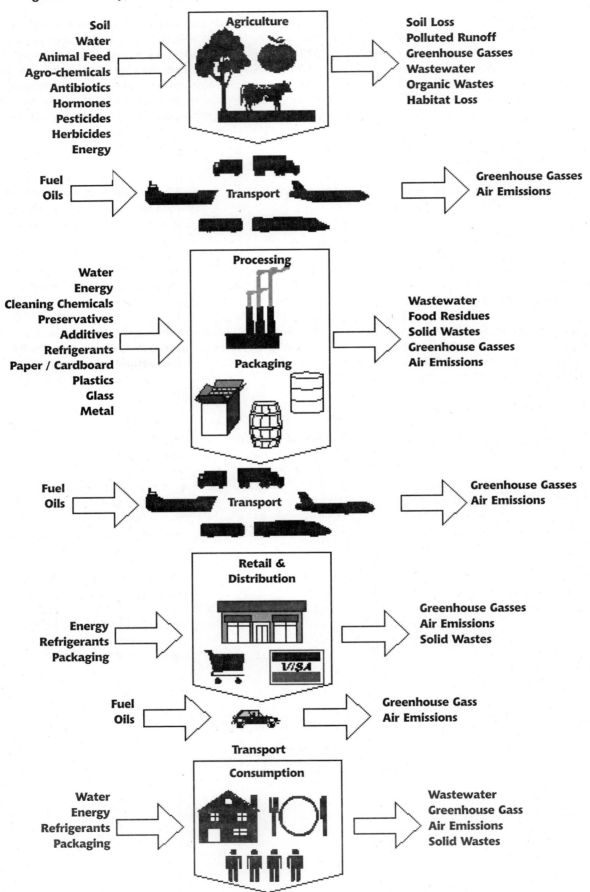

5.1.2 Circular food production systems

Although a large proportion of horticultural food products, for example, consumed in the UK are imported, marketed at supermarkets and purchased in shopping trips by car, there are many different options for fruit and vegetable cultivation, sourcing, distributing and marketing. For example, there are numerous ways in which fresh apples can be moved from the orchard (or individual apple tree) to a person's household. Apples can be home-grown, or sourced locally, nationally or imported and can be purchased packaged or unpacked at a range of retail outlets including supermarkets, greengrocers, outdoor markets, farmers' markets, farm shops or through home-delivery fruit and vegetable box schemes. The environmental impact will be different for each of these options. It is important to both consider food production (agriculture) and food distribution so that the environmental impact, both pre- and post-farmgate, can be compared (**see Section 3**).

For agricultural production systems in general to become less fossil-fuel-intensive implies reducing mechanisation and moving away from large scale, specialised production and the use of external inputs such as pesticides; synthetic fertilisers and veterinary drugs. Increasing the diversity and reducing the scale of food production systems are directly opposite to the current trends in commercial agriculture but are the goals of sustainable food production.[340]

Permaculture systems, one form of sustainable food production, are designed to minimise fossil fuel consumption, air and water pollution, solid waste and chemical residues in food, by developing 'closed loop' or 'circular' systems so that energy and material throughput is minimised (**Figure 17**). Local resources including renewable energy supplies, composted material and human labour replace fossil fuels, machinery, fertilisers and pesticides. Food production, based on organic, permaculture and other forms of low energy and resource input systems have, therefore, been proposed as sustainable approaches to meeting our food needs. However, sustainability also depends on what happens to the food products beyond the farm gate and, in particular, the distance between farm and consumer, the transport-related environmental costs and the degree of food processing and packaging.

Figure 17 Circular systems of food production, distribution and waste management[341]

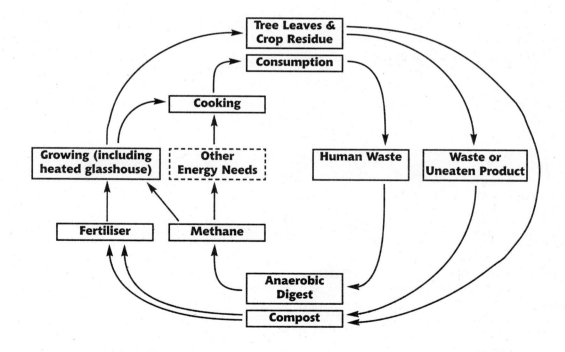

5.2 The organic food sector

In 1999/2000 the farm gate value for UK produced organic foods was £67 million, equivalent to 11 per cent of organic retail sales which amounted to £605 million. The European organic retail market was estimated to be worth £6 billion in 2000. In the UK, organic food sales more than doubled between the financial years 1997/1998 and 1999/2000 from £260 million to £605 million, which represented impressive annual growth rates of 40 per cent and 55 per cent (**Table 19**). UK organic retail sales are expected to exceed £1 billion in 2001.[342]

The rapidly expanding market for organic food has led the multiple retailers to recognise the potential of this sector and develop strategies to offer an ever widening range to their customers. As with conventional food products, the majority of organic foods are now purchased at supermarkets. In 1997/1998 the multiple retailers accounted for two-thirds of organic sales and their share increased to almost three-quarters in 1999/2000. Although there were 160 farmers' markets and 340 box schemes operating in the UK by 2000, the market share of these direct links between local producers and consumers declined in the two years to 2000 from 19 per cent to 13 per cent (**Table 19**). Sales at farm shops remained static between 1999 and 2000 mainly due to the impact of supermarket competition.[343]

Table 19 Organic food retail sales (£ million with percentage in brackets)[344]

	1997/1998		1998/1999		1999/2000	
Multiple retailers	175	(67)	269	(69)	451	(74)
Independent retailers & health food shops	36	(14)	63	(16)	78	(13)
Farmgate, box scheme & market stall	49	(19)	58	(15)	76	(13)
Total	260		390		605	

Although the area of UK agricultural land that was farmed organically or is in-conversion represented just 2.3 per cent of the total in April 2000, there was significant expansion between 1997 and 2000.[345] During this period there was a 7-fold increase in the area of land that is managed organically and the number of organic farms increased from 828 to 2,865.[346] However, almost nine-tenths of the area of land that has been converted to organic production in the UK is grassland (rough-grazing, temporary leys and permanent pasture), with organic arable and horticultural production amounting to only 10 per cent and 3 per cent, respectively. Even though horticulture represented such a small fraction of organically managed land in 2000, the farm gate value of fruit and vegetables was almost £25 million, 37 per cent of the total (**Table 20**).[347]

Table 20 Value of UK organic production, 2000

Product	Unit	Value (£m)
Fruit	3,655 tonnes	2.59
Cereals	37,600 tonnes	6.73
Meat	279,500 animals	8.05
Dairy	32.5 million litres	9.60
Eggs	177 million	18.00
Vegetables	121,020 tonnes	22.18
Total		67.14

Demand for organic food in the UK now far outstrips supply and this is why three-quarters of consumption comes from imports. One reason for this is the lack of support for farmers during and post-conversion. Another is that the majority of organic sales are at supermarkets and as discussed above, the multiple retailers require large volumes of year-round supplies and are reluctant to deal with local, small-scale food producers.

Comparing the energy consumed in transporting imported organic food to the energy saving of organic production over conventional production

Previously in this report it has been shown that the average energy saving of organic crop production over conventional cultivation is 0.68 MJ/kilogram of product. In **Table 21**, this average energy saving is compared to the transport energy consumption when importing organic horticultural produce. To determine the relative significance of transportation and different production techniques, the energy consumed when importing organic produce by road, sea and plane is divided by 0.68 MJ/kg.

Table 21 A comparison of the energy used during the production and distribution of organic food

Imports	Transportation Energy (MJ/kg food)	Transportation Energy / Energy Saving of Organic Production (0.68 MJ/kg)
New Zealand by plane	160.1	235
California by plane	74.6	110
Spain by road	1.7	2
New Zealand by ship	3.3	5
Argentina by ship	1.8	3

This ratio shows that the transport energy consumed when importing organic produce from southern Europe by truck is double the energy saving of organic over conventional production and five times greater when importing organic produce from New Zealand by ship. However, when organic produce is imported by plane from New Zealand, the transport energy consumption is 235 times greater than the energy savings of organic production.

It could be argued that if the growth in the organic sector had been achieved through farmers' markets and other forms of local food schemes, rather than through supermarkets, then organic food miles would be less of a problem. In a sustainable food system organic food would be available to all consumers, with the majority of foodstuffs sourced from within the locality or region.

To move towards this situation a two-pronged approach is needed to match the supply and demand for sustainably produced local food. These are:

1. Supply: accelerating the process of conversion to sustainable food production

At the moment British farmers that are eligible receive about £3 billion in CAP subsidies, while only about £20 million of government support is specifically directed to organic production. The UK government has not given strong enough support to promote organic production and therefore reduce the external costs of agriculture to the environment and human health.[348] The Soil Association, for example, believe that the considerably higher rates of conversion aid and post-conversion support offered in some EU countries, particularly for perennial fruit crops, is a cause of the low rate of conversion by fruit growers in the UK. An organic action plan[349] with a target of 30 per cent of UK agricultural land to be organic by 2010 is needed for the organic sector to ensure that:

- The organic sector develops sustainably rather than with the damaging boom and bust economic cycle so often seen in British farming.
- UK organic imports are reduced.
- Retailers can source more of their organic produce from the UK and thereby support British farmers.
- A level playing field for UK farmers develops as other European organic farmers benefit from greater Government support.
- Organic food becomes more accessible to people on low incomes.
- The confidence of the consumer in the food industry is rebuilt.

The conversion and diversification of farming could be combined with community food growing schemes and public sector initiatives. Urban food projects should also be encouraged so that the distance food is transported is minimised as 80 per cent of UK inhabitants live in cities or towns of over 10,000 people.

2. Demand: encouraging consumers to obtain food from sustainable systems

Although organic sales continue to grow rapidly, the sector is dependent on a small group of consumers who regularly purchase organic food. A third of all households do not make any organic purchases and of those that do, 30 per cent buy only one organic product a year. Less than 7 per cent of organic buyers account for 57 per cent of annual organic sales. It is clear that the organic market is polarised. Research by Taylor-Nelson/Sofres found that consumers who purchase organic food regularly tend to be "older, up-market buyers."[350] The main reason for not buying organic food is the cost compared to conventional produce. In a recent survey, 42 per cent of those respondents choosing not to eat organic said that they are put off by high prices.[351] Many more consumers would buy organic produce if it was more affordable. Supermarkets are partly responsible for the high price of organics and buying from alternative outlets, such as farmers' markets and box schemes tends to be cheaper (see **Box 6**). It also, of course, reduces the distances that food has travelled since such local distribution systems avoid imports and centralised distribution.

Other benefits of matching supply and demand on a local level

Although there are few relevant studies on local food and nutritional benefits, there is also evidence that where local food production is integrated with work to encourage healthier food consumption, there may be nutritional benefits. A survey was carried out of 275 people, who were members of community supported agriculture farms in Massachusetts. The dietary patterns of these people were compared with a control group. Fewer members used supermarkets, they shopped more in health food shops, and 82% of members reported an increase in the amounts of vegetables eaten compared with 39% of non-members.[352] Some evaluations have been reported by local food projects in the UK. For example, the 'Gardening For Health' allotments project in Bradford indicated an increase in fruit and vegetable consumption.[353]

In addition local food projects could offer the chance of obtaining good food at a low cost, and improve skills and confidence to try new foods and dishes.

However, if supermarkets continue to squeeze these alternative retail outlets consumers will be left with only two choices: high priced organic food from supermarkets or lower priced conventional food from supermarkets. Consumers on lower incomes are likely to have to make the latter choice, thus restricting the organic sector in a high price 'niche'.

Box 6 Organic price check

"The organic sector particularly suffers from this capture of value by certain stakeholder groups in the food system. It is commonly supposed that the higher prices consumers pay for organic produce is because growers find it more expensive to farm in an environmentally-friendly and welfare-conscious way. Sustainable agriculture does imply a shift of inputs away from pesticides and fertilisers to knowledge, management skills and labour. However, a surprisingly small proportion of the premium paid by consumers gets back to farmers. In Denmark, for example, organic producers receive a tenth more for their milk compared with conventional producers, but the price in the supermarkets is 32 per cent higher. The same is true for wheat - farmers receive 80 per cent more for organic wheat, but organic flour costs 100 per cent more. The extra value is captured almost entirely by distribution and profits" Jules Pretty.[354]

Research into the price difference between conventional and organic food has found that the premium for organic produce averages 64 per cent.[355] However, this hides large variations across the 250 items included in the survey: 285 per cent on carrots; 158 per cent on cheese; 11 per cent on baby food. Purchasing a range of organic food at a supermarket cost £145 compared to £90 for the non-organic alternatives. The products chosen included fruit and vegetables, meat and poultry, and a wide range of groceries. But alternative retail outlets such as farmers' markets were found to offer a better deal. Prices of organic meat and poultry were 37 per cent higher in local supermarkets than at Bristol Farmers' Market and organic vegetables were 33 per cent more expensive.[356] These lower prices make organic food more attractive to a wider range of consumers and offer the potential for the organic sector to break out of its niche into the mainstream.

5.3 Diversify production to shorten the food chain

Regional specialisation in agriculture has already occurred in many industrialised countries, with large areas of land producing only a few different types of, or a single, crop or livestock. The US is a prime example with wheat prairies, enormous cattle ranches and large factory-style pig production facilities. Even in the UK, specialisation means that over 40 per cent of bulb onion and carrot production is in East Anglia, the majority of brussels sprouts, cauliflower, calabrese and winter cabbage are cultivated in Lincolnshire and over half the apple, pear and cherry orchards are in Kent.[357] With Southern countries also moving to specialised production for export there are now concerns about what is being lost in terms of biodiversity, traditional livestock and crop varieties, and indigenous knowledge (**Section 4.6**).

This increasingly specialised agriculture and production for export inevitably leads to longer distances between producers and consumers. Specialised food production for export has also been associated with industrialised agriculture in which the environmental damage associated with the manufacture and supply of inputs increases.[358]

This process could be reversed by re-establishing local and regional food supply systems and substituting 'near for far' in production and distribution systems. This would reduce both the demand for and the environmental burdens associated with transportation. Minimising the distance between product source and consumer implies local food production and homegrown produce which in turn has implications for a very wide range of government policies. Britain was, however, virtually self-sufficient in food during the Second World War and in recent years there has been a resurgence of interest in allotments, farmers' markets and local organic food producer/consumer links.[359]

Progress is being made in many areas of the UK in terms of local food production, marketing and composting schemes.[360] In Wye, Kent domestic and business 'waste' is now separated and either composted or recycled. Each household now produces only 100 kg of waste per year (the national average is 1000 kg); local businesses have cut waste by 75% and savings of £10,000 have been made.[361] The project is co-ordinated by Richard Bowden of WyeCycle and aims to 'go full circle' so that composted material is returned to local gardens and farms.[362] Food produced locally is marketed at farmers' markets and through box schemes and local wholesalers, which minimises food transportation and packaging and farmers have responded to strong demand by diversifying. The aim of diversification is two-fold – an increase in the number of different foods and varieties of each, and the provision of food throughout the year. One farm in the region can now supply a range of fruit and vegetables all year round. It offers over a hundred different varieties of apples as well as a selection of plums, pears, cob nuts and other fruits and vegetables. WyeCycle is now looking at other aspects of local sustainability including food wastes, and renewable energy generation, possibly in the form of a wind turbine.[363]

5.4 Applying the proximity principle: comparing local and global sourcing

"Why do local farmers attempt to sell their produce into a non-specified, anonymous and distant market when there may be 12,000 people, including schools and local authority canteens, needing to be fed right on their doorstep? 'Adding value' and local retailing stimulate 'pride of place and pride of product' and encourages a further closing of the current yawning gap between producer and consumer" Julian Rose.[364]

The proximity principle is a straightforward concept in which production processes are located as near to the consumer as possible. When applied to food supply, local food systems in the form of home-delivery box schemes, farmers' market and shops selling local produce would replace imported and centrally distributed foodstuffs. There are obvious environmental benefits in terms of reduced transportation and also economic gains (**see Section 5.4**).

"Britain imports 61,400 tonnes of poultry meat from the Netherlands in the same year that it exports 33,100 tonnes of poultry meat to the Netherlands. Britain imports 240,000 tonnes of pork and 125,000 tonnes of lamb while exporting 195,000 tonnes of pork and 102,000 tonnes of lamb."[365]

Taking UK food supply and trade at present, there is great potential to apply the proximity principle, in the form of import substitution. Apart from products such as bananas, coffee and tea, many of the foodstuffs that are imported at present could be produced in Britain. For example, seasonal availability in the UK, the move to specialised production of fewer varieties of each product, the expectation of year round availability and strict cut-off dates for UK sourcing of particular food products by the multiple retailers are some of the reasons why certain fresh foods are now imported in large quantities. However, many meat products, cereals, dairy products and cooking oils are or could be available here throughout the year. This could also apply to fruit and vegetables, perhaps the most seasonal of food groups, through a combination of cultivating different varieties and traditional and modern storage and preservation techniques. As the example above in Wye, Kent showed, the decision to supply local markets, to diversify and to focus on extending seasonal availability has led to the year round supply of many fresh products including apples.

Similarly, the land currently used to produce food that is exported could be used to increase our self-sufficiency. The example of how Cuba has increased self-sufficiency in food is given in **Box 7**. **Table 22** shows foodstuffs for which the quantity produced in the UK is very close to the amount consumed in the UK. Despite this, there are significant levels of imports and exports in these products at present, including over 5.3 million tonnes of milk, 6.5 million tonnes of wheat and 2 million tonnes of meat products.

Table 22 UK food production and trade for five food categories, 1998 (1000 tonnes)[366]

	Production	**Imports**	**Exports**	**Domestic Use**
Wheat	15470	1844	4663	13551
Pulses (such as Peas and Beans)	701	167	186	682
Meat	3733	1408	649	4492
Dairy products	464	350	252	587
Milk	14635	3029	2266	15451

In the UK, to achieve both a balanced diet and a more sustainable food system, there needs to be a shift away from meat and dairy products to the consumption of more fruit, vegetables and cereals.[367] If fruit, vegetable and cereal consumption in the UK is to increase without increasing carbon dioxide emissions, and other forms of environmental damage, then self-sufficiency in these products will also need to rise. In 1998 these food products accounted for over half of all food imports by weight. At present, a large proportion of the overall UK food trade gap is accounted for by imports of fruit and vegetables, for example, in 1996 these products accounted for 50 per cent of the UK food trade deficit by value.

There are therefore three significant benefits associated with the conversion of livestock enterprises to mixed farms or the cultivation of crops, combined with a move away from food production for export to import substitution. These are: a healthier diet; reduced environmental damage; and an increased and more sustainable income for farmers.

There is also growing evidence of the even greater environmental benefits of local sourcing of food in terms of reduced transport related environmental impact. In the case of organic produce, **Figure 18** compares local and global sourcing of produce marketed in different outlets. The results are based on a survey of retailers between June and August 2001. Products were chosen that were available in the UK during these months but are at present imported by the multiple retailers. These include:

■ Imports by plane - spring onions (Mexico – 8941km)
■ Imports by road - potatoes (Sicily – 2448km)
■ Imports by ship – onions (New Zealand – 18839km)

The results show the transportation of these products from their source to a consumer's home. If the consumer walks or cycles to a farm shop to purchase the product then there will be no transport impact. Home delivery box schemes and independent retailers are also environmentally efficient when produce is sourced locally or regionally, as are farmers' markets, particularly when shopping is not by car. However, if the product is imported and purchased at a supermarket there will be four transport stages, resulting in carbon dioxide emissions of between 249 and 5298 grammes per kilogram of product. When imported by plane the environmental impact increases significantly, as this stage alone results in over 5kg of CO_2.

If locally sourced spring onions were bought through a home delivery box scheme, there would be 300 times less carbon dioxide emissions than if they were imported by plane 9,000 kilometres from Mexico and purchased in a shopping trip by car at a supermarket.

Figure 18 The carbon dioxide emissions of organic food sourcing, distribution and marketing systems (grammes of CO_2 per kilogram product)[368]

	To Britain	To Wholesale / Distribution Centre	To Store	To The Home
Source Mexico **Total CO2** 5298 **Outlet** Multiple Retailer	5069	13	6	183
Source Sicily **Total CO2** 356 **Outlet** Multiple Retailer	154	13	6	183
Source New Zealand **Total CO2** 431 **Outlet** Multiple Retailer	230	13	6	183
Source Regional **Total CO2** 195 **Outlet** Independant S'market			12	183
Source Local **Total CO2** 17 **Outlet** Box Scheme				17
Source Local **Total CO2** 187 **Outlet** Farmers' Market			12	183
Source Local **Total CO2** 183 **Outlet** Farm Shop				183

Other studies show how local food systems can help the economy as well reduce food miles and allow a direct transaction between the food producer and consumer:

■ A New Economics Foundation (NEF) study has shown that money spent on locally-produced food generates almost twice as much income for the local economy as the same amount spent in a typical supermarket. The finances of a Cornish vegetable box scheme, Cusgarne Organics, based near Truro were tracked in a survey. The study followed the trail of income to monitor exactly where its turnover was spent, how much of it was spent locally, what happened to this money at the next level of spending and so on. It was found that every £10 spent with a local food initiative is worth £25 for the local area, compared with just £14 when the same amount is spent in a supermarket. The same amount is worth more with local schemes as it stays in the vicinity, where its value increases as it is reinvested many times over.[369]

■ The local food sector in Devon, Somerset and Dorset includes 900 businesses involved in food production, processing, wholesaling, retailing and catering. The farms employ an average of 3.4 full time jobs, compared to an average of 2.34 full time jobs for the South West as a whole, so that, in all, that there are 954 more jobs in agriculture. On average these businesses spend £30,000 per year in the local economy, a total of £27 million per annum.[370]

■ Farmers' markets offer produce that is locally produced and customer surveys show that the public are keen to support their local producers. Supporting local food production and marketing boosts local employment and income. As Roger Thompson from Business in the Community, Cornwall points out "we estimate that in Cornwall, £500 million per year is spent on food. Seventy-five per cent of that food is imported from outside Cornwall. If we can reduce that by just one per cent, we have invested £5 million in our local economy".

■ 40,000 households in the UK receive a box of organic produce, delivered to their door each week. The largest box scheme, Riverford, based in Devon, delivers 3500 boxes of organic vegetables per week. These are fresh vegetables direct from the farm and at lower than supermarket prices.

■ In Austria, 50 municipalities are now moving towards sustainable production and consumption through a programme of `pro-local supply'. This aims to encourage the consumption of locally produced goods and services (particularly food). There have been a number of positive spin-offs in terms of reduced transport and economic regeneration.[371]

■ West Devon Environmental Network found that there was a massive demand for local organic produce which far exceeds the available supply. They have estimated that if this demand was met by local producers it could add £4.9 million to the local economy every year, and create at least 61 new jobs. WestDEN co-ordinated the first farmers' market to be held at Tavistock, which was a great success and have recommended that farmers' markets should be encouraged to allow locally-grown foods to be sold locally in an accessible way.[372]

Many of the above examples involve organic produce as the those supplying organic and those demanding organic have tended towards more direct relationships which also reduce food miles. However, not all organic food is locally produced and it is worth comparing the energy consumed in long distance organic distribution to the energy saving of organic over conventional food production (**Section 5.2**).

Box 7 Building up self-sufficiency and sustainability in Cuba.

Cuba has developed one of the largest organic agriculture systems in the world, and organic farmers from other countries are now visiting the island to find out more about the innovative techniques that have been developed. Prior to the 1990s, Cuba had followed a typical pattern of colonial food production: cultivating luxury export crops while importing food for its own people. In 1990 over 50 per cent of Cuba's food came from imports. The withdrawal of Soviet aid in 1989 meant that 1,300,000 tons of chemical fertilisers, 17,000 tons of herbicides, 10,000 tons of pesticides and farm machinery could no longer be imported, and highly industrialised, fuel and capital-intensive farming practice came to an end.[373] Cuba lost 85 per cent of its foreign trade, including food, agricultural imports and petroleum. Already crippled by the U.S. embargo, the country was financially devastated with its food supply hit hardest.

Cuba needed to find an alternative to high-input monocultural production. The state's priorities shifted to create "the largest conversion from conventional agriculture to organic or semi-organic farming that the world has ever known." [374] One of Cuba's responses was to develop urban agriculture. Planting in the city as well as in the countryside, reduced the need for transportation, refrigeration, and fossil fuels. By 1998 there were over 8000 urban farms and community gardens run by over 30,000 people in and around Havana, with production growing at 250-350 per cent per year. Today, food from the urban farms is grown almost entirely with active organic methods as the use of chemical pesticides in agriculture within city limits is prohibited. The quality of fresh produce from production has improved and yields have increased and production costs have been reduced.[375] The state also created farmers markets, which legalised direct sales from farmers to consumers, and many now operate around the city on the garden sites.

At first, sustainable agriculture was seen as the only option following the withdrawal of Soviet support. When they began this effort, most policy-makers could not imagine any significant amount of rice being grown in Cuba without the conventional chemical inputs. But by 1997 small-scale rice production had reached 140,000 tons, 65 per cent of national production. According to official figures, in 1999 organic urban agriculture produced 65 per cent of Cuba's rice, 46 per cent of the fresh vegetables, 38 per cent of the non-citrus fruits, 13 per cent of the roots, tubers, and plantains, and 6 per cent of the eggs.[376] Production is based on interplanting where diverse crops are planted together, which discourages the pests that accompany monocrop farming. Imported fertiliser has been replaced with 173 'vermicompost' centres, which produce 93,000 tonnes of natural compost a year.[377] The state is supporting the new urban gardeners through extensive university research into sustainable organic practices and Cuba's scientific community is also developing biological fertilisers and pesticides using naturally occurring organisms and insects.

Although Cuba is organic by default because it has few means of acquiring pesticides and herbicides, so far Cuba has been successful with its transformation from conventional, high-input, mono-crop agriculture to a more diverse, and localised farming system. The country is rapidly moving away from a monoculture of tobacco and sugar. It now needs much more diversity of food crops as well as regular crop rotation and soil conservation efforts to continue to properly nourish millions of Cuban citizens. Cuba provides an inspirational model not only for sustainable food production but a complete sustainable food system.

6) How do we create a sustainable food system?

"One cannot solve a problem with the same kind of thinking that created it" Albert Einstein.[378]

The political climate is changing. Food and farming issues have never had such a high profile or been the focus of so many concerns. Some countries are now reviewing their food and agricultural policies with the aim of becoming more sustainable. However, very few governments are addressing the underlying causes of the many problems that have been associated with the contemporary food system.

6.1 The role of government

During the foot and mouth crisis of 2001, the UK Prime Minister promised a radical overhaul of farming and the "armlock" that the multiple retailers had over it. The new Department for Environment, Food and Rural Affairs (DEFRA) and the Cabinet Office announced an independent Food and Farming Commission to look at the sustainability of this sector.

Unfortunately, there is currently little sign of serious questioning of the fundamental causes of the series of food and farming crises. This is exemplified in the documentation intended to initiate a debate on the future of food and farming in the UK. There is, for example, a striking dichotomy at the heart of the consultation document published by the new Department for Environment, Food and Rural Affairs (DEFRA) and in the terms of reference for the Policy Commission on Food and Farming.[379] [380]

"To advise the Government on how we can create a sustainable, competitive and diverse farming and food sector which contributes to a thriving and sustainable rural economy, advances environmental, economic, health and animal welfare goals, and is consistent with the Government's aims for CAP reform, enlargement of the EU and increased trade liberalisation" Department for Environment, Food and Rural Affairs.[381]

Although Government aims to reform the CAP and to create a sustainable food and farming system, the Government also aims to increase trade liberalisation in food, which translates into the UK farming becoming ever more 'internationally competitive'. This will inevitably mean larger farms, industrialised production and increased transportation. If barriers to trade in food are reduced, farm incomes and the number of farmers in the UK are likely to continue to decline as a result of cheap imports.

Moreover, there is no evidence to show that further trade liberalisation will result in sustainable food supply chains, thriving rural economies and improved human health. The evidence presented in this report shows that the reverse is more likely to be true. Unfortunately, this evidence is rarely taken seriously.[382] Even more worrying is the impression that the UK Government, and perhaps a majority of countries across the world, are now so locked into the process of ever more globalisation, through treaties and trading blocks, that they are no longer able to introduce policies that could bring about a sustainable food system.

What this means in effect is that even if import substitution and a move to local food production for local consumption are shown to be the only way to achieve sustainability, the government is powerless in terms of introducing policy measures that allow them to become more widespread. Maybe Mr. Blair is in an armlock as well as UK farmers.

More encouraging is the fact that the new department which covers food and farming issues also has key strategic priorities to: [383]

- safeguard the continuing availability to the consumer of adequate supplies of wholesome, varied and reasonably priced food and drink;
- encourage the development of local products;
- find ways of preventing future animal, plant and fish disease outbreaks;
- promote more sustainable management and use of natural resources (e.g. energy) in the UK and internationally; and
- play a leading role in seeking international agreement on climate change and move towards the goal of reducing UK carbon dioxide emissions to 20 per cent below 1990 levels by 2010.

However, these objectives will not be realised if there is increased UK food transport and the emphasis remains on the ability of farmers to compete internationally. In the case of carbon dioxide emissions, the target may be met under current accounting methods. However, in the case of UK food supply, it is unlikely that this 20 per cent reduction would be achieved if the carbon dioxide emissions associated with food imports, resulting from production and processing in the country of origin and international freight transport were included.

The alternative scenario is one in which food is sustainably produced and distributed. This would require international trade in food to be minimised, the CAP to be replaced by a policy aimed at promoting sustainable food production in the UK (and other EU countries) and direct support and targets for local and regional food schemes (**see Box 8** on the EU sustainable development strategy).

Box 8 Sustainable development in Europe?

European leaders finally adopted the first ever EU sustainable development strategy in Gothenburg in June 2001.[384] The strategy is substantially weaker than the draft presented by the European Commission and focuses on objectives for sustainability without setting concrete targets or deadlines for action.[385] In practice, any specific proposal from the Commission's paper that had been opposed by any single member state was dropped. Germany has opposed an end to fossil fuel subsidies, the UK has opposed road pricing, Italy and Greece have opposed curbs on tobacco subsidies, and France has reservations on suggested changes to the Common Agricultural Policy. Most of the specific policies proposed by the European Commission have not been taken up by European leaders and EU environment commissioner Margot Wallström expressed disappointment that leaders had not been *"more specific on concrete actions."* [386]

The European Commission has proposed an initial list of six headline indicators to monitor the implementation of the strategy. The indicators were chosen to reflect four priority action areas: climate change, transport, public health and natural resources. Total greenhouse gas emissions, the energy intensity of the economy, transport intensity of economic output, shifts in the modal split of transport, urban air quality, and municipal waste generation will be measured and presented in a "synthesis report" on progress at the Spring Heads of State council in Barcelona in 2002. At this meeting the Commission has stated that they would like to focus on climate change and transport issues.

The EU aims to "decouple economic growth from resource use" by implementing an integrated product policy. However, the environmental dimension of the EU sustainable development strategy is accompanied by the economic target to become the most competitive region in the world.[387] As discussed earlier, a focus on food production will be inadequate if the need to become ever more internationally competitive alongside reducing food miles (in this instance intra- and extra-EU food transport) is not addressed.

6.2 Complementary approaches to re-localising the food supply

The value of UK food, feed and drink imports in 1999 was over £17 billion. It is clear that a reduction in food imports through import substitution would not only be of benefit to the UK economy as a whole but could also be a major driver in rural regeneration as farm incomes would increase substantially. Local food systems also have great potential to reduce the damaging environmental effects of the current food supply system. There are essentially three mechanisms through which the food system could relocalise. These are:

     a) Voluntary approaches by the agriculture and food industries and consumers;
     b) Increases in environmental taxes; and
     c) Targets and direct policy and fiscal support for local food systems.

a) Voluntary approaches by the agriculture and food industries and consumers

Although many multiple retailers now have a local sourcing policy and even targets for the percentage of food products sourced within the locality or region, a recent survey by Sustain found that very little local, seasonal produce is to be found on supermarket shelves.[388] Out of 2075 products surveyed, only 79 (4 per cent) were locally sourced. As discussed earlier, even when supermarkets promote produce as being local or regional, the food will probably have been transported a considerable distance due to regional distribution centres and centralised processing. The targets that have been set for local sourcing by the multiple retailers are low. Asda, for example, aims to source two per cent of food products locally. At present local food sourcing is largely a public relations exercise for major retailers unless local is interpreted as British or regional as being sourced in Scotland, Wales or the South West of England.[389] The economies of scale and centralised distribution systems of the multiple retailers are simply not suited to dealing with small-scale producers and direct deliveries to stores by local farmers and processors.

Pressure from customers and increased purchasing of local produce at supermarkets could alter the situation but many consumers remain unaware of the significance of food miles. Many of those who are concerned about the long-distance distribution of food may already shop at farmers' markets or receive a home-delivery box scheme. However, information could be improved through some form of label which indicates the distance accumulated and the transport-related environmental impact (**Figure 19**). For imported produce the mode of transport for the longest leg in the supply chain could appear on the label in the form of an icon (e.g. ✈ if imported by plane). Alternatively, the transport effects could be represented in the form of a scale from 1-10 (with 1 representing local produce delivered to the home and 10 for produce imported from New Zealand by plane). Colour coding could also be applied e.g. green for local, orange for UK sourced and red for imported produce. The organic certifier Bio-Swiss already distinguishes between imported and national produce on the label.

Labelling of this kind would need to be accompanied by a leaflet containing further information and an explanation, together with useful websites. In a recent survey of consumers, 59 per cent of respondents said they always or usually refer to labelling information.[390] In the same survey 18 per cent of respondents stated that they usually looked at the country of origin on labelling, only 6 per cent said that food labels contain too much information and a third said more information could be added to food labels without causing problems.

Many restaurants, hotels and public houses now source ingredients locally. This is often seen as a direct way to support local farmers and also indicates the freshness and seasonality of the food on the menu. The National Trust now has a policy to supply its restaurants and cafeterias with local food. This is a welcome move that could become more widespread.

b) Increases in environmental taxes

Another way to reduce the damaging effects of food miles is to increase the costs of transportation so that the environmental damage (such as air pollution and greenhouse gas emissions) that is described as 'external costs' are accounted for. In Switzerland, a Heavy Vehicle Fee (HVF) was introduced in January 2001, as a result of a successful public referendum passed in 1998.[392] The HVF charges heavy goods vehicles (over 3.5 tonnes) based on their gross weight, kilometres driven and emissions. Billing for most vehicles is based on data from an electronic on-board data collection unit that records vehicle mileage and route. At the end of each month the data are transmitted to the Swiss Customs Agency either by mail or electronically. This information is used to generate a bill, similar to other utilities.

Figure 19 Examples of environmental labels for fresh produce[391]

The 1999 White Paper *Sustainable Distribution: A Strategy* raised the possibility that in the future vehicle excise duty on UK lorries may partly reflect their environmental impact.[393] The Department for Transport, Local Government and the Regions (DTLR) has acknowledged that '*congestion is increasingly common on the trunk road and motorway network*' and is '*forecast to get worse*'. The case for trying to ease congestion by expanding road capacity has been largely rejected, with emphasis placed instead on making better use of existing road space and more effectively managing demand.[394] However, the strategy places more emphasis on various methods to improve the efficiency of freight transport in order to minimise congestion, make better use of transport infrastructure, manage development pressures and reduce the negative environmental impact of freight movement.[395] The emphasis is on making existing supply chains more sustainable and on continued economic growth. The localised alternatives are not considered. The problems of road freight are tackled as they may affect economic growth and it is economic growth that will pay for the damage caused by the increases in freight which are a direct result of economic growth.[396]

Efficiency gains are limited and tend to be offset by increases in freight demand. As a result this approach will not bring about the 70 per cent cut in carbon dioxide emissions that is now required.

In 1994, the Royal Commission on Environmental Pollution recommended that fuel duty be increased every year so as to double the price of fuel, relative to the prices of other goods, by 2005, which would require a 9 per cent annual increase in fuel duty.[397] The Commission advocated a 20 per cent reduction in carbon dioxide emissions from surface transport between 1990 and 2020 and estimated that a 9 per cent annual increase in fuel price would be sufficient to achieve this, but would need to be monitored. Successive UK governments adopted increases in fuel duty as the principal measure for limiting increases in carbon dioxide emissions from road transport until the fuel protests in 2000, following which the fuel duty escalator was dropped. In fact it was in effect reversed in the April 2001 budget when significant concessions were made to road hauliers and motorists. The annual budget introduced cuts in road fuel and vehicle taxes amounting to £1.7 million, with fuel tax reduced by 4p a litre and a large reduction in vehicle licenses on lorries.[398]

It is assumed that increases in the costs of road transport will encourage a shift to more environmentally benign modes of transport such as rail freight, and public transport and home delivery in the case of shopping trips that are currently done car. In theory, if transport costs continue to increase there will be a point at which existing distribution systems become uneconomic and alternative distribution systems that are more localised become a viable alternative.

The problem with this approach is that there will be strong public resistance to increased road transport costs, and in the case of the food system such moves will be resisted by some farmers, and most road hauliers and the multiple retailers. The other concern is the timescales involved, as it could take 10 years or more for increases in fuel costs above the rate of inflation to take effect and for more localised supply chains to become widespread.

Although a return to the fuel price escalator is currently seen as being politically unacceptable, its reintroduction will be required if sustainable food supply is to become a reality. However, local food schemes will need to be developed at the same time and preferably beforehand in order provide an attractive and viable alternative to transport-intensive food supply chains.

c) Targets and direct policy and fiscal support for local food systems

Developing a sustainable food system should now become a key policy objective for central government, local government and regional development agencies, based on targets for sustainable food production, import substitution, fair trade and local sourcing of food. For instance, the initiative recently announced to provide 'one piece of fruit per school child' offers an ideal opportunity for the government to show its commitment to the development of a sustainable food system. Ambitious targets could be set to meet this increased demand in fresh fruit locally.

Funds available at local, regional, national and European (Rural Development Regulation) level should be directed to support the development of sustainable local and regional food distribution systems.

Specifically, there should be an increase in siphoning of CAP production subsidies into support for sustainable farming, up to the allowable 20 per cent. The measure should be tapered so that the measure is targeted at those who can afford it. The Treasury must be encouraged to match the funds freed in this way to support a far wider programme of agri-environment and rural development schemes. All farmers, for instance, should have access to appropriately set, whole farm stewardship payments, regional food economies should be encouraged and CAP price support and export subsidies phased out. Regional Development Agencies could also play an important role in developing regional food systems though grant allocation, technical support and marketing advice. All regional development plans should include local food economy targets.

Localised food sourcing, distribution and retailing schemes that are less dependent on transport, although increasing in number, still represent only a small fraction of food sales in the UK and could not cover any shortfall in food supplies as a result of oil supplies being cut or a large increase in the price of oil. Farmers' markets, box schemes and urban agriculture are viable but will expand significantly only if supported directly. If this happens then the 'norm' that we have today could quite quickly be replaced by sustainable food schemes.

Local Authorities are now considering the potential of local food schemes and are looking at ways in which local food can be promoted.[399] Direct support for the expansion of local food systems could come in the form of targets set for the procurement of local food by schools, hospitals and publicly run catering facilities. The targets could be modest to begin with, which would allow local food producers to adapt to the new circumstances. Another mechanism that could be used is inducement through the tax system, so that the rates paid by businesses such as hotels, restaurants and caterers would be reduced if a certain percentage of their food is supplied locally or regionally.

The many farm assurance schemes, such as organic, which now exist should take the lead by introducing the proximity principle into certification. The options for reducing the damaging effects of post-farm gate transport by providing incentives to market produce locally, for example, through reduced certification costs or an added premium or market advantage should now be considered.

Although this report has explained the benefits of and the obstacles to the development of a more localised food system, more research is needed. This should be undertaken by an independent body and involve stakeholders in developing the terms of reference and methodology. The changes required in the process of localising the food system in terms of diversification, extending seasonal availability and storage techniques also require further research. Regional demonstration centres and local centres of excellence to provide examples of best practice and act as demonstration and educational centres also merit exploration. The introduction of practical and classroom based education on food, farming and sustainable development in the National Curriculum would also help to raise awareness and understanding.

7) Conclusions

The contemporary food system is inherently unsustainable. Indicators of social, environmental and economic performance, such as food security, greenhouse gas emissions, food miles, farm income and biodiversity highlight this fact. Indeed, in many respects we are moving away from the goal of ensuring supplies of safe and affordable food with minimum environmental impact while providing a secure living for food producers. Whilst organic farming has increased, leading to significant environmental benefits, increased organic food imports have created additional burdens on the environment. This reports reveals why we should not continue with these trends in the food system.

A sustainable food system cannot rely, almost completely, on one finite energy source; an energy source which causes enormous levels of pollution during its production, distribution and use. Although food supplies in wealthy countries such as the UK appear to be secure and choice, in terms of thousands of food products being available at supermarkets, seems limitless, this is an illusion. The vulnerability of our food system to sudden changes was demonstrated during the fuel crisis in 2001. A sharp increase in the price of oil or a reduction in oil supplies could present a far more serious threat to food security. Food production and distribution, as they are organised today, would not be able to function. Moreover, the alternatives, in the form of sustainable agriculture and local food supplies, which minimise the use of crude oil, are currently unable to respond to increased demand due to low investment and capacity.

This report has shown that food distribution is now a significant contributor to climate change. Climate change is predicted to affect food production across the globe. To reduce the threat of reduced yields or even crop failure, the significant carbon dioxide emissions associated with food distribution must be reduced by minimising the distance between producer and consumer. The greenhouse gas emissions associated with international trade must be accounted for so that they can be included in reduction targets. Airfreight, which has particularly damaging environmental effects, should be phased out altogether. Taxing aviation fuel would be a start.

We also cannot ignore the other, significant problems associated with the long distance transport of food. Other pollutants from the transport system, spread of disease, poor animal welfare, and reduced nutritional quality are all significant.

The current emphasis on sustainable agriculture alone is and will continue to be inadequate. There are many benefits to organic farming, including reduced fossil fuel energy consumption and greenhouse gas emissions. However, these are often overshadowed by the environmental damage of long distance transport. Organic products that are transported long distances, particularly when distribution is by plane, are almost as unsustainable as their conventional airfreighted counterparts. Highly processed and packaged organic foodstuffs have an even greater environmental impact and are even less sustainable.

In poorer countries, food (and natural resource) production for export has been associated with increased poverty, displacement, reduced local food security and a dependency on a one or a few commodities for which prices have fluctuated significantly. If food production in the South continues to become increasingly intensive, requiring high levels of external inputs then the safety of farm workers and environmental and economic sustainability will be at higher risk. Worse still, if climate change accelerates, countries in the South will be severely affected, including their ability to produce food. Instead of continuing with this system we should aim, instead, to convert to fair trade products that cannot be produced in the UK, and to import these products by ship, the least damaging mode of inter-continental transport.

The priority, for both North and South, in terms of food security must be the development of local and regional food systems in which a large percentage of demand is met within the locality or region. This approach, combined with fair trade, will ensure secure food supplies, minimise fossil fuel consumption and reduce the vulnerability associated with a dependency on food exports (as well as imports). Localising the food system will require significant diversification and research into forgotten plant and animal varieties and sustainable food production techniques. Putting the theory of 'circular food systems' into practice will need the investment and support that has, so far, not been forthcoming.

Local food schemes, such as farmers' markets, fruit and vegetable box schemes, and processing and adding-value on or close to the farm have been shown to contribute to a thriving rural economy. These schemes also provide an assured market close by, stable rural employment and a sense of certainty for producers allowing experimentation, diversification and the investment that are intrinsic to sustainable development. Unfortunately, many in the food and farming sector who would benefit from this shift to sustainable production are dissuaded from doing so due to the uncertainty within the contemporary food system. The need to reduce costs in order to be competitive does not allow food producers to get off the treadmill and plan ahead.

The government says it is serious about sustainable development, including sustainable food and farming. If so, it must seriously reconsider its commitment to further trade liberalisation in food and services related to food.

More trade means more food transport, more oil consumption and, therefore, all the environmental and social damage associated with it, which we have set out in this report. We have also shown how this damage could be avoided, and how positive economic, social and environmental outcomes - which go to the heart of sustainable development - can be achieved through a sustainable food system. All we need now is action.

8) Recommendations for action

The following six key action points summarise our recommendations. More detailed policy proposals are made below:

- Developing a sustainable food system should become a major government policy based on setting targets for sustainable food production, import substitution, fair trade and local sourcing of food to be achieved over a specific period.
- Measures should be introduced to internalise the external environmental and social costs of transportation to minimise the damaging effects of international and national food freight transport by air and road and shopping by car.
- Agricultural support policies should be redirected specifically to promote sustainable food production and localised food sourcing and processing.
- Fiscal measures such as tax incentives should be introduced to encourage businesses and public sector bodies to buy food from local or regional suppliers.
- Labelling on all food products should be introduced to indicate the environmental impact of distribution. Organic and other assurance schemes should take the lead by introducing the proximity principle into certification.
- More research is urgently required into the obstacles to and benefits from changing to a localised food system.

Consumers can have a huge influence over the food industry. Purchasing decisions in the shops can make a difference to the way food is produced and to how far it travels before it is bought. Although there is now a far greater awareness of the issues, there is also an even greater urgency to address the problem of ever increasing food miles. As progress has been limited, we feel justified in reiterating several of the recommendations from the original Food Miles Report together with other action that must now be taken. A Contact List is given to assist those wanting to take further action.

1 What individuals can do: help to increase real choice

1.1 When buying food that can be grown in the region, i.e. Europe, individuals could follow a hierarchy of purchasing priorities:
    i. buy locally produced food (which should therefore be seasonal);
    ii. buy nationally;
    iii. buy from the region.

1.2 When buying food that cannot be grown in the region, such as tea, coffee, bananas, or chocolate, individuals should buy fair trade products where these are available.

1.3 Consumers should try to buy locally produced, seasonal fresh produce when available, from small, local shops and markets, and request that produce be stocked from farms in the surrounding area. This can be ensured by purchasing food at farmers' markets, community supported agriculture schemes and in many instances through box schemes.

1.4 Individuals could investigate setting up their own local produce marketing scheme or join an existing one [see Soil Association in Contacts List].

1.5 People could consider opportunities for growing their own food, in gardens or allotments or supporting local food growing initiatives, for instance in community gardens or city farms.

1.6 Individuals could write to their MP and MEP, to the DEFRA and the Food Standards Agency and to supermarkets and food manufacturers, demanding a clear labelling system showing the distance food has travelled, its country or countries of origin and transport-related environmental impact.

1.7 Ask retailers how food products have been imported and avoid those products that have involved airfreight distribution.

1.8 Individuals can ask publicly funded canteens (such as schools, hospitals, care homes, meals on wheels, local authority, Government agencies and armed forces) to buy more food locally from organic suppliers.

2 What farmers and growers can do: develop sustainable food production.

2.1 The farming sector should examine the potential to market produce locally [see Contacts List].

2.2 Diversifying production for local consumption, and introducing more value-adding of foods on-farm such as part- or whole-processing could increase farm incomes.

2.3 Consider working more co-operatively with other local and regional food producers to market produce and share skills and machinery.

3 What organic and other assurance scheme providers can do: provide sufficient information to allow the public to choose food products that are truly sustainable.

3.1 Considering the significant environmental burdens associated with airfreight imports, UK organic certifiers should follow the lead of Bio-Swiss, for example, and reconsider the certification of products imported and exported by plane.

3.2 The International Federation of Organic Agricultural Movements (IFOAM) and national certifiers should introduce the proximity principle into standards and certification and consider the inclusion of post-farm gate environmental effects in the labelling of organic produce. This could cover processing, packaging and transportation, although data on the environmental impact of processing and packaging is currently difficult to obtain.

3.3 The many farm assurance schemes that now exist should also consider options for reducing the damaging effects of post-farm gate transport by providing incentives to market produce locally, for example, through reduced certification costs or an added premium or market advantage.

4 What food retailers and processors can do: move away from international sourcing and centralised distribution

4.1 Retailers and manufacturers should give priority to: sourcing locally; avoiding airfreight; transporting more food by rail and inland waterway; reducing overall fuel consumption; and stocking fair trade products. Targets should now be set by retailers for local and national sourcing as part of plans to reduce the length of supply chains. Greater local autonomy in purchasing within supermarket chains can allow for more local sourcing and greater regional diversity.

4.2 Retailers and processors should introduce national labelling schemes for fresh and processed products showing food miles, the country/countries of origin and the environmental impact of distribution. In the case of retailers, itemised till receipts should show country/countries of origin of foods and an indicator of the environmental damage of distribution.

4.3 Reusable packaging schemes should be (re-)introduced. This will be facilitated through local and regional food sourcing systems.

4.4 DEFRA and the meat industry need to support the development of decentralised and/or mobile abattoirs which can reduce the distance that animals have to travel, stress and food miles.

5 What the food service sector can do: buy ingredients from local sustainable suppliers

5.1 Catering companies should give priority to sourcing locally, transporting more food by rail freight, reducing overall fuel consumption, avoiding food imported by plane and using fair trade products.

5.2 Catering companies should introduce national assurance and labelling schemes for food ingredients and products showing food miles, the country/countries of origin and the environmental impact of distribution. Menus and information displays should also show this type of information.

6 What Local Authorities can do: encouraging the development of sustainable food schemes across the UK

6.1 Targets should be set for the proportion of food in the public sector such as at schools, hospitals, and canteens that is supplied locally.

6.2 Business rates could be scaled so that caterers, restaurants, public houses, hotels etc. that source a proportion of their food locally would obtain a rebate.

6.2 Existing powers (Planning Policy Guidelines 6 and 13 for example) should be used to encourage and revitalise small, local and/or high street shops, and local markets.

6.3 A more rapid development of local farmers' markets, box schemes and community supported agriculture should be encouraged.

6.4 The land use planning system, through structure plans or unitary development plans, should be used to control the sitings of supermarkets and centralised distribution facilities.

7 What national and devolved government can do: take sustainable development seriously

7.1 As part of a climate change policy, the climate change levy should be expanded to include the greenhouse gas emissions associated with imports (i.e. the production-related emissions within the country exporting the product) and trade-related transportation should be included in the Kyoto Protocol.

7.2 Minimising the damaging effects of food miles through the local sourcing of food should be encouraged directly through the tax system so that companies that minimise the life cycle environmental impact of the products which they market are penalised less.

7.3 Funds available at local, regional, national and European level (such as CAP and Objective 1 funding) should be used to directly support the sustainable development of local and regional food distribution systems.

7.4 Regional Development Agencies could also play an important role in developing regional food systems though grant allocation, technical support and marketing advice. All regional development plans should include local food economy targets.

7.5 Targets should be set for import substitution, fair trade and local sourcing to be achieved over a specific period. This would require an analysis of unnecessary trade at present and the potential and change required to move to localised food production and distribution.

7.6 More research is urgently required into the benefits of and the obstacles to the development of a more localised food system. The changes required in the process of localising the food system in terms of diversification, extending seasonal availability and storage techniques also requires further research; regional demonstration centres; and local centres of excellence to provide examples of best practice and act as demonstration and educational centres. This could be co-ordinated by a single body to represent the local food sector in the UK.

7.7 Measures must be introduced to reduce the long-distance transport of foods, particularly air and road freight. These should include: a lorry weight-distance tax to ensure the heavier more damaging traffic is costed properly; the reintroduction of the of the fuel duty escalator to ensure distribution becomes more environmentally efficient through a shift to rail, water and local sourcing; and introducing a much needed tax on aviation fuel. The revenue should be ear-marked not only for environmentally less damaging transport schemes but also for alternative local sourcing systems such as farmers' markets, community supported agriculture and box schemes.

7.8 Similarly, the environmental cost of food production should be accounted for so that damaging effects are reduced and gradually eliminated. The revenue from a pesticide tax, for instance, which could raise £84-131 million pounds a year[400], could be hypothecated to encourage research into, and directly support, sustainable food production. Again such taxes would need to be phased in over, say, a 10 year period.

7.9 Small and medium sized abattoirs and other food processing facilities that are decentralised should also be given direct support to ensure that they provide the high standard facilities needed for a regional food system. This could reduce the distance that animals have to travel, stress during transit and food miles.

7.10 Products should be required to carry information to consumers to show the country/countries of origin for fresh and processed foods, the distance imported, and the mode of transportation used.

7.11 Assistance should be provided for localised direct marketing schemes, such as information on how to set them up and to obtain cheap loans or grants.

7.12 Food From Britain should be restructured and its remit altered so that its primary emphasis is on import substitution not export promotion.

7.13 Aid and debt-relief for poor countries should be linked to sustainable development initiatives such as diversification, sustainable agricultural production and environmental protection. The Government should lobby international agencies such as the IMF and the World Bank to implement multilateral debt-relief and promote sustainable agriculture.

7.14 Pressure should be exerted for the multilateral adoption of minimum standards for working conditions, environmental protection, and animal welfare in the production of goods and services, at both European and international levels. This could be achieved through reform and democratisation of the WTO. If these changes are not forthcoming, the government should call for the formation of a World Environment Organisation, as recommended by the Government Panel on Sustainable Development.

7.15 Education on sustainable food and farming, both practical and classroom-based, should become a central feature of the National Curriculum. Food production at schools, combined with visits to farms, community food projects and farmers' markets could be combined with home economic lessons in which ingredients are produced at the school or are sourced locally (and will therefore be in season).

7.16 Government's widely praised scheme to provide a free piece of fruit each day for all 4-6 year olds by 2004 would be enhanced by further targets to include vegetables, and a rising proportion of produce to be purchased locally from sustainable supplies.

References

[1] Steven Shrybman, *Trade, agriculture and climate change*. Institute of Agriculture and Trade Policy, November 2000.

[2] MAFF, 2001. *Energy use in organic farming systems*. ADAS Consulting for MAFF, Project OF0182, DEFRA, London.

[3] Waste Watch, 2001. *Recycling for householders*. Waste Watch at www.wastewatch.org.uk

[4] Based on data from - FAO Food Balance Sheet Database, 2001, at www.fao.org

[5] FAO Food Balance Sheet Database, 2001, at www.fao.org

[6] The Soil Association, 2001. *The organic food and farming report 2000*. The Soil Association, Bristol

[7] Cowell, S., and R. Clift., 1996. *Farming for the future: an environmental perspective*. Paper presented at the Royal Agricultural Society of the Commonwealth, July 1996, RASC.

[8] Data for shipping and airfreight from *Guidelines for company reporting on greenhouse gas emissions*. Department of the Environment, Transport and the Regions: London, March 2001. Data for trucks is based on Whitelegg, J. (1993) *Transport for a sustainable future: the case for Europe*. Belhaven Press, London and Gover, M. P. (1994) *UK petrol and diesel demand: energy and emission effects of a switch to diesel*. Report for the Department of Trade and Industry, HMSO, London.

[9] DETR, 2000. *Focus on Ports*. Department of the Environment Transport and the Regions, HMSO, London

[10] DETR, 2000 *The Future of aviation: the Government's consultation document on air transport policy*. Department of Environment, Transport and the Regions, London.

[11] Brendon Sewill, 2000. *Tax free aviation*. Aviation Environment Federation, December 2000.

[12] Jones, J. A., 1999. *The environmental impacts of distributing consumer goods: a case study on dessert apples*. PhD Thesis (unpublished). Centre for Environmental Strategy, University of Surrey, Guildford, Surrey, UK.

[13] DETR, 1999. *Transport statistics Great Britain*. Department of the Environment Transport and the Regions, HMSO, London.

[14] Medea – European Agency for international information,2001. *Oil Reserves*. at - http://www.medea.be/en/

[15] Joe Quinlan, 1997. *Oil: Asia and Oil - Three Numbers for Investors to Contemplate*. Morgan Stanley, New York, 13 June 1997 at www.morganstanley.com

[16] DETR, 2001. *The draft UK climate change programme*. HMSO, London.

[17] RCEP, 2000. *Energy – the changing climate*. 22nd Report of the Royal Commission of Environmental Pollution, The Stationery Office, London.

[18] Committee on the Medical Effects of Air Pollutants, 1998. *Quantification of the Medical Effects of Air Pollution in the United Kingdom*. HMSO, London

[19] British Marine Life Study Society, 2001. *Oil Tanker Disasters: Oiled Bird Count*. at http://ourworld.compuserve.com

[20] Bender and Bender, 1997. *Nutrition Reference Handbook*. Oxford University Press

[21] MAFF, 1996. *Manual of Nutrition*. 10th Edition. The Stationery Office, London.

[22] RAFI, 1997. *Human Nature: Agricultural biodiversity and farm-based food security*. Rural Advancement Foundation International for the FAO. Ottawa, Canada

[23] Eurostat, Statistical Office of the European Community.

[24] UNCTAD, 2000. *Least developed countries report 2000*. United Nations Commission on Trade and Development, New York and Geneva.

[25] FAO Food Balance Sheet Database, 2001

[26] H. Barrett et. al., 1999. Globalisation and the changing networks of food supply: the importation of fresh horticultural produce from Kenya into the UK. *Transactions of the Institute of British Geographers*. Vol 24 p159-174

[27] Human Rights Watch, 1999. *The Price of Oil*, Human Rights Watch, New York.

[28] Matthieu Calame and Philippe Cacciabue, 2000.*The European rural world and sustainability*. Framework text of the topic, Europe Working Group Forum, The Alliance for a Responsible, United and Plural World. at http://www.alliance21.org/continental/en/europe/forums_rur_ref.htm

[29] See Böge, S., 1993. *Road Transport of Goods and the Effects on the Spatial Environment*. Wupperthal Institute, Germany; Paxton, A., 1994. *The Food Miles Report: The Dangers of Long Distance Food Transport*. The SAFE Alliance, London; Kranendonk, S. and Bringezu, S., 1993 *Major Material Flows Associated with Orange Juice Consumption in Germany*. Wupperthal Institute, Germany; Whitelegg, J. (1995) *Freight Transport, Logistics and Sustainable Development*. WWF, Godalming.

[30] Sustain, 2001. *Local food sourcing – PR or the real thing?, unpublished report*, A survey by Sustain, April 2001

[31] Brewster Kneen, 1993. *From land to mouth: understanding the food system, Second Helping*. NC Press

[32] See Böge, S., 1993. *Road Transport of Goods and the Effects on the Spatial Environment*. Wupperthal Institute, Germany; Paxton, A., 1994. *The Food Miles Report: The Dangers of Long Distance Food Transport*. The SAFE Alliance, London; Kranendonk, S. and Bringezu, S., 1993 *Major Material Flows Associated with Orange Juice Consumption in Germany*. Wupperthal Institute, Germany; Whitelegg, J. (1995) *Freight Transport, Logistics and Sustainable Development*. WWF, Godalming.

[33] NFU, 1999. *Ham from deer and margarine from cows?* Press Releases, 15th June 1999, National Farmers Union, UK.

[34] NFU, 1999. *British Public 'hungry' for British food*. Press Releases, 10th May 1999, National Farmers Union, UK.

[35] Blythman, J., 1998. *The food we eat (second edition)*. Penguin Books, London and Pretty, J. N. 1998. *The living land: agriculture, food and community regeneration in the 21st Century*. Earthscan, London.

[36] Kneen, B., C. McDougall, and C. Kneen. 1997. *A baseline for food policy in British Columbia*. FarmFolk/CityFolk Society Vancouver, British Columbia.

[37] NFU, 2001. *NFU farming factsheet*. National Farmers Union, UK.

REFERENCES

38 NFU, 2001. *NFU farming factsheet.* National Farmers Union, UK.

39 Connon, J.M and Schiek, W. A., 1997. *Food Processing: an Industrial Powerhouse in Transition.* Wiley, London.

40 Hird, V., 1999. *Food Miles-still on the road to ruin,* 1999, Sustain: the alliance for better food and farming.

41 FSA, 2001. *Consumer attitudes to food standards.* Final Report, Prepared for the Food Standards Agency and COI Communications by RSGB, January 2001.

42 FT, 2001. *Lex Column.* Financial Times Website at FT.com, April 11th 2001

43 Caroline Lucas, 2001. *Stopping the Great Food Swap - Relocalising Europe's food supply.* Green Party, 2001

44 Pretty, J. N., 1998. *The living land: agriculture, food and community regeneration in the 21st Century.* Earthscan, London and Caroline Lucas, 2001. *Stopping the Great Food Swap - Relocalising Europe's food supply.* Green Party, 2001

45 Pretty, J, N, Brett, C, Gee, D. Hine, R.E, Mason, C.F. Morrison J.I.L, .Raven, H, Rayment, M.D, Van der Bijl, G, An assessment of the total external costs of UK agriculture, *Agricultural Systems* (65)2 (2000) pp. 113-136, UK, 2000.

46 Caroline Lucas, 2001. *Stopping the Great Food Swap - Relocalising Europe's food supply.* Green Party, 2001

47 Elliot, V. 2000. Panic buyers force stores to ration food. *The Times.* September 14th 2000. Times Newspapers Ltd. London.

48 Pretty, 2001. *Taking Back the Middle for Farmers and Communities.* Extract from Jules Pretty. 1998. *The Living Land: Agriculture, Food and Community Regeneration in Rural Europe.* At www.essex.ac.uk/ces

49 Pretty, 2001. *ibid*

50 Pretty, 2001. *ibid*

51 Sustain, 1999. *A Battle in Store.* Based on data from *The Impact of Out-of-centre Food Superstores on Local Retail Employment.* Porter S, Raistrick P. Occasional Paper No 2. The National Retail Planning Forum Nottingham, 1998.

52 Julian Rose, 1998.Countryside, What Countryside? *Permaculture Magazine* No. 23

53 Mark Muller, Catherine Hofman and Paul Hodges, 2000. *Addressing Climate Change and Providing New Opportunities for Farmers.* Institute for Agriculture and Trade Policy, Minnesota, USA, September 2000

54 Green, B. M., 1978. *Eating Oil - Energy Use in Food Production.* Westview Press, Boulder, CO. 1978.

55 Weizsäcker, E. U. von, Lovins, B., and Lovins, L. H., 1998. *Factor Four: Doubling Wealth, Halving Resource Use.* Earthscan, London.

56 Jones, J. A., 1999. *The environmental impacts of distributing consumer goods: a case study on dessert apples.* PhD Thesis (unpublished). Centre for Environmental Strategy, University of Surrey, Guildford, UK.

57 Mark Muller, Catherine Hofman and Paul Hodges, 2000. *Addressing Climate Change and Providing New Opportunities for Farmers.* Institute for Agriculture and Trade Policy, Minnesota, USA, September 2000

58 Based on data on sourcing from UKROFS and a survey of supermarket stores during June – August 2001; distance tables for air miles at www.indo.com/cgi-bin/dist and the environmental impact of airfreight in *Guidelines for company reporting on greenhouse gas emissions.* Department of the Environment, Transport and the Regions, London, March 2001.

59 *ibid*

60 *ibid*

61 Julian Rose, 1998. Countryside, What Countryside? *Permaculture Magazine* No. 23, Permaculture Association.

62 Based on data on sourcing from UKROFS and a survey of supermarket stores during June – August 2001; distance tables for air miles at www.indo.com/cgi-bin/dist and the environmental impact of freight transport in *Guidelines for company reporting on greenhouse gas emissions.* Department of the Environment, Transport and the Regions: London, March 2001.

63 Steven Shrybman, 2000. *Trade, agriculture and climate change.* Institute of Agriculture and Trade Policy, Minnesota, USA, November 2000.

64 FAO, 2001. *Food Balance Database. 2001.* Food and Agriculture Organisation, Rome at www.fao.org

65 Energy use in organic farming systems ADAS Consulting for MAFF, Project OF0182,, DEFRA, London, 2001

66 *Harmonisation of environmental life cycle assessment for agriculture.* Final Report, 1997, Concerted Action European Commission DG VI Agriculture, Brussels.

67 Energy use in organic farming systems ADAS Consulting for MAFF, Project OF0182, DEFRA, London, 2001

68 Energy use in organic farming systems ADAS Consulting for MAFF, Project OF0182, DEFRA, London, 2001

69 Energy use in organic farming systems ADAS Consulting for MAFF, Project OF0182, DEFRA, London, 2001

70 *Regenerating Agriculture: Policies and practice for sustainability and self-reliance.* Pretty, J. N. 1995, Earthscan, London.

71 *The environmental impacts of organic farming in Europe.* M. Stolze et. al. Organic Farming in Europe: Economics and Policy, Volume 6, Stuttgart University, Germany, 2000.

72 *Packaging.* Waste Watch at www.wastewatch.org.uk

73 *Top 10 Wacky Waste Facts!* Waste Watch at www.wastewatch.org.uk

74 *Recycling for householders.* Waste Watch at www.wastewatch.org.uk

75 *Environmental impact of packaging in the UK food supply system.* Industry Council on Packaging and the Environment, 1996, London.

76 John Vidal, 2001. Food redistribution. *The Guardian,* Society, 24th October 2001.

77 *Plastics.* Waste Watch at www.wastewatch.org.uk

78 Sasha Norris, 2000. Waste that we want not - Why we need to end our obsession with plastic wrapping. *The Guardian. Wednesday August 16, 2000.*

79 Waste Watch at www.wastewatch.org.uk

REFERENCES

80   *Recycling for householders.* Waste Watch at www.wastewatch.org.uk

81   *Recycling for householders.* Waste Watch at www.wastewatch.org.uk

82   *Plastics.* Waste Watch at www.wastewatch.org.uk

83   Andersson, K. Ohlsson, P and Olsson, P. 1996, *Life Cycle Assessment of Tomato Ketchup.* The Swedish Institute for Food and Biotechnology, Gothenburg.

84   Kooijman, J. M. 1993. Environmental assessment of packaging: sense and sensibility. *Environmental Management* 17(5):575-586.

85   Kooijman, J. M. 1993. Environmental assessment of packaging: sense and sensibility. *Environmental Management* 17(5):575-586.

86   Jones, J. A., 1999. *The environmental impacts of distributing consumer goods: a case study on dessert apples.* PhD Thesis (unpublished). Centre for Environmental Strategy, University of Surrey, Guildford, Surrey, UK.

87   Carried out by Sustain in the South-East of England in several stores during June-August 2001

88   Based on data from *Transport Statistics for Great Britain: 2000 Edition.* Department of the Environment, Transport and the Regions, and port distance tables at http://www.distances.com

89   Carlsson, A. 1997. *Greenhouse gas emissions in the life-cycle of carrots and tomatoes. IMES/EESS Report No. 24,* Department of Environment and Energy Systems Studies, Lund University, Sweden.

90   *Transport Statistics for Great Britain: 2000 Edition.* Department of the Environment, Transport and the Regions.

91   DTI, 1995. *Energy Paper 65: Energy Projections for the UK.* Department of Trade and Industry, HMSO, London.

92   DETR. 1997. *Transport statistics for Great Britain.* Department of the Environment Transport and the Regions, HMSO, London.

93   DETR, 1999. *Tackling climate change in the UK.* Department of the Environment Transport and the Regions, HMSO, London, 1999.

94   Tim Lang and Colin Hines, 1993. *The new protectionism: protecting the future against free trade.* Earthscan

95   World Bank, 1997. *Global economic prospects and the developing countries, 1997.* World Bank, Washington DC.

96   FAO, 2001. *Food Balance Database. 2001.* Food and Agriculture Organisation, Rome at www.fao.org

97   FAO, 2001. *Ibid*

98   FAO, 2001. *Ibid*

99   FAO, 2001. *Ibid*

100   Caroline Lucas, 2001. *Stopping the Great Food Swap - Relocalising Europe's food supply.* Green Party, 2001

101   Caroline Lucas, 2001. *ibid*

102   Lobstein, T, and Hoskins, R, *The Perfect Pinta.* Food Facts No. 2. The SAFE Alliance, 1998.

103   FAO, 2001. *Food Balance Database. 2001.* Food and Agriculture Organisation, Rome at www.fao.org

104   A. and J. Gear, 2001. *Viewpoint. The Organic Way,* Issue 163, Spring 2001, Henry Doubleday Research Association

105   Natasha Walter, 2001. When will we get the revolution. *The Independent* 19th July 2001

106   The Soil Association, 2001. *The organic food and farming report 2000.* The Soil Association, Bristol

107   The Soil Association, 2001. *ibid*

108   NFU representative in the Guardian, 4.1.99

109   Based on data from Raven, H., Lang, T. and Dumonteil, C., 1995. *Off Our Trolleys: Food Retailing and the Hypermarket Economy.* Institute of Public Policy Research, London and MAFF, 1998. *Basic Horticultural Statistics for Great Britain.* Ministry of Agriculture, Fisheries and Food. various years between 1939 and 1998, HMSO, London

110   BBC, 2001. *Crisis in the Countryside.* Panorama (transcript) BBC, Sunday 1 April 2001

111   BBC, 2001. *Crisis in the Countryside.* Panorama (transcript) BBC, Sunday 1 April 2001

112   SFFA, 2001. *Farmers unable to make a living – information on 6 supermarket products predominantly or solely produced in the UK.* Small and Family Farmers Alliance, Cornwall, 6/4/2001.

113   The Soil Association, 2001. *The organic food and farming report 2000.* The Soil Association, Bristol

114   Out of this World, 2001. *Unethical Organics.* Out of this World News, Issue 14, Spring 2001.

115   The Soil Association, 2001. *The organic food and farming report 2000.* The Soil Association, Bristol

116   The Soil Association, 2001. *ibid*

117   Lawrence Woodward, David Fleming and Hardy Vogtmann, 1997. Health, sustainability and the global economy: The organic dilemma. *Elm Farm research Centre Newsletter,* 1997. A paper originally given in the 11th IFOAM conference in Copenhagen, Denmark, August 1996.

118   A. and J. Gear, 2001. Viewpoint. *The Organic Way,* Issue 163, Spring 2001, Henry Doubleday Research Association

119   Data for shipping and airfreight from *Guidelines for company reporting on greenhouse gas emissions.* Department of the Environment, Transport and the Regions: London, March 2001. Data for trucks is based on Whitelegg, J., 1993. *Transport for a sustainable future: the case for Europe.* Belhaven Press, London; and Gover, M. P., 1994. *UK petrol and diesel demand: energy and emission effects of a switch to diesel.* Report for the Department of Trade and Industry, HMSO, London.

120   Jones, J. A. 1999. *The environmental impacts of distributing consumer goods: a case study on dessert apples.* PhD Thesis (unpublished). Centre for Environmental Strategy, University of Surrey, Guildford, Surrey, UK

121   Jones, J. A. 1999. *ibid*

122   Raven, H., Lang, T. and Dumonteil, C., 1995. *Off Our Trolleys: Food Retailing and the Hypermarket Economy.* Institute of Public Policy Research, London

123   Raven, H., Lang, T. and Dumonteil, C., 1995. ibid.

REFERENCES

[124] Based on data from the Vehicle Certification Agency at www.vca.gov.uk; Whitelegg, J., 1993. *Transport for a sustainable future: the case for Europe.* Belhaven Press, London; and Gover, M. P., 1994. *UK petrol and diesel demand: energy and emission effects of a switch to diesel.* Report for the Department of Trade and Industry, HMSO, London.

[125] Simms, A, Kumar, R. and Robbins, N., 2000. *Collision course: free trade's free ride on the global climate.* New Economics Foundation, London

[126] Simms, A, Kumar, R. and Robbins, N., 2000. *ibid*

[127] Cowell, S., and R. Clift., 1996. *Farming for the future: an environmental perspective.* Paper presented at the Royal Agricultural Society of the Commonwealth, July 1996, CES, University of Surrey.

[128] DETR, 2000. *Focus on Ports.* Department of the Environment Transport and the Regions, 2000

[129] DETR, 2001. *Major ports of United Kingdom, by mode of appearance: 1999 (Foreign and domestic traffic),* Transport Statistics, Maritime statistics: United Kingdom. Department for Transport, Local Government and the Regions, The Stationary Office, London, 2001.

[130] DETR, 2000. *Focus on Ports.* Department of the Environment Transport and the Regions, 2000

[131] DETR, 2000. ibid

[132] DETR, 2000. *Transport statistics Great Britain.* Department of the Environment Transport and the Regions, HMSO, London.

[133] DETR, 2000. *Focus on Ports.* Department of the Environment Transport and the Regions, 2000

[134] DETR, 2000. *ibid*

[135] ENDS, 2001. *Transport becoming less not more sustainable. ENDS Environment Daily,* Issue 1057, 11th September 2001.

[136] ENDS, 2001. EU sustainable development strategy adopted. *ENDS Environment Daily,* Issue 1011 Monday 18th June 2001

[137] Simms, A, Kumar, R. and Robbins, N., 2000. *Collision course: free trade's free ride on the global climate.* New Economics Foundation, London

[138] J.M.W. Dings, W.J. Dijkstra and R.C.N. Wit., 1997. *European aviation emissions: trends and attainable reductions.*Report of background study, December 1997, Centre for Energy Conservation and Environmental Technology, Delft, The Netherlands.

[139] J.M.W. Dings, W.J. Dijkstra and R.C.N. Wit., 1997. *ibid*

[140] Chris Hewett, 2001.*Clear Air.* Green Futures, May/June 2001, Forum for the Future.

[141] Brendon Sewill, 2000. *Tax free aviation.* Aviation Environment Federation, December 2000.

[142] DoT, 1991. *UK airfreight 1980-1990.* Department of Transport. HMSO, London.

[143] DETR, 2000. *The Future of aviation: the Government's consultation document on air transport policy.* Department of Environment, Transport and the Regions, HMSO, London

[144] DETR, 2000. *ibid*

[145] DoT, 1991. *UK airfreight 1980-1990.* Department of Transport. HMSO, London.

[146] DETR, 2000. *The Future of aviation: the Government's consultation document on air transport policy.* Department of Environment, Transport and the Regions, HMSO, London

[147] DETR, 2000. *Transport statistics Great Britain.* Department of the Environment Transport and the Regions, HMSO, London.

[148] Brendon Sewill, 2001. Is the aviation industry sustainable. *Inside Track,* Summer 2001.

[149] Brendon Sewill, 2000. Tax free aviation. *Aviation Environment Federation,* December 2000.

[150] Brendon Sewill, 2000, ibid

[151] Brendon Sewill, 2000, ibid

[152] Environmental Health, 2001. *EU wants green tax to improve air quality.* The Official Journal of the Chartered Institute of Environmental Health, 2nd March 200, London, UK.

[153] Chris Hewett, 2001. *Clear Air.* Green Futures, May/June 2001, Forum for the Future.

[154] Francis Vanek, 1999. Sustainably Distributed? An environmental critique of the UK Government's 1999 White Paper on Distribution. *World Transport Policy and Practice,* Volume 6, Number 2, 2000, at www.ecoplan.org/wtpp

[155] DETR, 2000. *Transport statistics Great Britain.* Department of the Environment Transport and the Regions, HMSO, London.

[156] DETR, 1999. *Sustainable Distribution: A Strategy* Department of the Environment, Transport and the Regions, 1999, at www.dtlr.gov.uk

[157] DETR, 1999. *Transport statistics Great Britain.* Department of the Environment Transport and the Regions, HMSO, London.

[158] Jones, J. A. 1999. *The environmental impacts of distributing consumer goods: a case study on dessert apples.* PhD Thesis (unpublished). Centre for Environmental Strategy, University of Surrey, Guildford, Surrey, UK.

[159] DETR, 1999. *Transport statistics Great Britain.* Department of the Environment Transport and the Regions, HMSO, London.

[160] DETR, 1999. *Transport of Goods by Road 1998,* Department of the Environment Transport and the Regions, HMSO, London

[161] DETR, 1999. *Transport statistics for Great Britain.* Department of the Environment Transport and the Regions, HMSO, London.

[162] Raven, H., T. Lang,. and C. Dumonteil. 1995. *Off our trolleys: food retailing and the hypermarket economy.* Institute of Public Policy Research, London.

[163] BRE, 1998. *Building a sustainable future.* General information report 53, energy efficiency best practice programme, Building Research Establishment.

[164] DETR, 2000. *Transport Statistics Bulletin.* National Travel Survey: 1997/99 Update, HMSO, London.

[165] Hamer, M., 1993. City Planners against Global Warming. *New Scientist,* 24 July 1993.

[166] DETR, 2001. *The draft UK climate change programme.* DETR, 2001. HMSO, London.

[167] ENDS, 2001. EU climate policy package delayed. *ENDS Environment Daily,* 1083, 17th October 2001

REFERENCES

[168] Anthony Sampson, 2000. We're on the brink. *The Guardian*, 17th October 2000 p19.

[169] Campbell, 2001. *The Oil Peak: A Turning Point.* Solar Today July/August 2001 C.J. Campbell at www.solartoday.org

[170] The Guardian, 2001. We're on the brink. *The Guardian*, 17th October 2000 p19.

[171] Colin J. Campbell, 1997. *The Coming Oil Crisis.* Multi-Science Publishing Co. Ltd

[172] Energy Information Agency. From http://environment.about.com/library/weekly/aa092700.htm

[173] Medea: European Agency for International Information, 2001. *Oil Reserves.*at - http://www.medea.be/en/

[174] Anthony Sampson, 2000. We're on the brink. *The Guardian*, 17th October 2000 p19.

[175] Carl Mortished, 2000. Memories of Gulf War send oil markets into a panic. *The Times*, October 13th 2000

[176] EIA, 2001. *World Oil Market and Oil Price Chronologies: 1970 – 2000.* Department of Energy's Office of the Strategic Petroleum Reserve, Analysis Division, Energy Information Administration, Department of the Environment, USA, at www.eia.doe.gov

[177] Matthew Jones, 2001. Analysis: Which way now for global oil prices? *Financial Times*, September 21 2001.

[178] Colin J. Campbell, 1997. *The Coming Oil Crisis.* Multi-Science Publishing Co. Ltd

[179] Green Party USA, 2001. *World crude oil reserves – Statistical information.* Based on data from the Oil and Gas Journal and the Energy Information Agency. At http://environment.about.com/library/weekly/aa092700.htm

[180] Green Party USA, 2001. *ibid*

[181] Medea: European Agency for International Information, 2001. *Oil Reserves.* at - http://www.medea.be/en/

[182] David Fleming, 2001. *The Great Oil Denial. Submission to the UK Energy Review.* At http://www.cabinet-office.gov.uk/innovation/2001/energy/submissions/Fleming.

[183] Medea: European Agency for International Information, 2001. *Oil Reserves.* at - http://www.medea.be/en/

[184] DTI, 2001. *Development of UK Oil and Gas Resources (the "Brown Book").* Various issues. Department of Trade and Industry. The Stationery Office, London

[185] Joe Quinlan, 1997. *Oil: Asia and Oil - Three Numbers for Investors to Contemplate.* Morgan Stanley, New York, 13 June 1997 at www.morganstanley.com

[186] Paul Brown, 2001. Melt Down *The Guardian*, Society July 18th 2001

[187] DETR, 2000.*Quality of life counts.* Department of the Environment Transport and the Regions, HMSO, London.

[188] Paul Brown, 2001. *Melt Down* The Guardian, Society July 18th 2001

[189] Forum for the Future, 2001. *Annual Report.* Forum for the Future, London

[190] RCEP, 2000. *Energy – The Changing Climate.* The Royal Commission on Environmental Pollution, Twenty-second Report, June 2000, HMSO, London.

[191] American Association for the Advancement of Science, 2001. *Atlas of population and environment.* University of California Press

[192] DETR, 2001. *The draft UK climate change programme.* Department of Environment, Transport and the Regions, HMSO, London.

[193] Mark Muller, Catherine Hofman and Paul Hodges, 2000. *Addressing Climate Change and Providing New Opportunities for Farmers.* Institute for Agriculture and Trade Policy, Minnesota, USA, September 2000

[194] Marland, G., T.A. Boden, and R. J. Andres, 2001. *Global, Regional, and National Fossil Fuel CO2 Emissions. In Trends: A Compendium of Data on Global Change.* Carbon Dioxide Information Analysis Center, Oak Ridge National Laboratory, U.S. Department of Energy, Oak Ridge, Tenn., U.S.A.

[195] USDOE, 2001.*World Carbon Dioxide Emissions from the Consumption and Flaring of Fossil Fuels, 1980-1999.* US Department of the Environment at http://www.eia.doe.gov/pub/international/iealf/tableh1.xls

[196] RCEP, 2000. *Energy – The Changing Climate.* The Royal Commission on Environmental Pollution, Twenty-second Report, June 2000, HMSO, London.

[197] ENDS, 2001. EU climate policy package delayed. *ENDS Environment Daily* Issue 1083, 17/10/01

[198] ENDS, 2001. EU sustainable development strategy adopted. *ENDS Environment Daily*, Issue 1011 Monday 18th June 2001

[199] ENDS, 2001. ibid

[200] RCEP, 2000. *Energy – The Changing Climate.* The Royal Commission on Environmental Pollution, Twenty-second Report, June 2000, HMSO, London.

[201] DETR, 2001. *The draft UK climate change programme.* DETR, 2001. HMSO, London.

[202] RCEP, 2000. *Energy – The Changing Climate.* The Royal Commission on Environmental Pollution, Twenty-second Report, June 2000, HMSO, London.

[203] Robert Engelman, 1998. *Profiles in Carbon: An Update on Population, Consumption and Carbon Dioxide Emissions.* Population Action International website at http://www.populationaction.org

[204] USDOE, 2001.*World Carbon Dioxide Emissions from the Consumption and Flaring of Fossil Fuels, 1980-1999.* US Department of the Environment at http://www.eia.doe.gov/pub/international/iealf/tableh1.xls

[205] DETR, 2001. *The draft UK climate change programme* DETR, HMSO, London.

[206] RCEP, 2000. *Energy – The Changing Climate.* The Royal Commission on Environmental Pollution, Twenty-second Report, June 2000, HMSO, London.

[207] BRE, 1998. *Building a sustainable future.* General information report 53, energy efficiency best practice programme, Building Research Establishment, Garston, UK.

[208] OECD, 1999. *OECD Environmental Data.* Organisation for Economic Cooperation and Development

209 DETR, 2001. *The draft UK climate change programme* DETR, HMSO, London.

210 Forum for the Future, 2001. *Annual Report.* Forum for the Future, London

211 Environmental Health, 2001. Failure to assess health effects of global warming. Environmental Health Journal p6 4/5/2001

212 Forum for the Future, 2001. *Annual Report.* Forum for the Future

213 Hadley Centre for Climate Prediction and Research, 1999. *Climate change and its impacts: stabilisation of CO2 in the atmosphere.* The DETR/Met Office.

214 DETR, 2001. *The draft UK climate change programme* DETR, HMSO, London.

215 Environmental Health, 2001. Failure to assess health effects of global warming. *Environmental Health Journal* p6 4/5/2001

216 DETR, 2001. *The draft UK climate change programme* DETR, HMSO, London.

217 DETR, 2001. *ibid*

218 DETR, 2001. *ibid*

219 NFU, 2001. *NFU farming factsheet.* National Farmers Union, 2001.

220 BBC, 2001. *Grain prices hit consumers.* BBC website on 31 August 2001 at
http://www.bbc.co.uk/liverpool/news/2001/08/31/dough.shtml

221 *Agra Europe,* 2001. Greek crops to get artificial rain. May 18th 2001

222 Reuters, 2001. *Global warming to hit key food crops.* based on Reuters News Service, November 8, 2001. *at*
http://www.planetark.org/dailynewsstory.cfm/newsid/13168/story.htm

223 Reuters, 2001. *ibid*

224 RCEP, 1994. *Transport and the Environment.* 18th Report of the Royal Commission on Environmental Pollution. 1994, HMSO, London.

225 Ball, D. J., 1991. *Review of air quality criteria for the assessment of near field impacts of road transport.* UK Transport Research Laboratory

226 CMEAP, 1998. *Quantification of the Medical Effects of Air Pollution in the United Kingdom.* Committee on the Medical Effects of Air Pollutants, HMSO, London

227 FOE, 1999. *Road Transport, Air Pollution and Health.* FoE Briefing, Friends of the Earth, March 1999

228 FOE, 1999. *ibid*

229 DETR, 2000. *Transport Statistics for Great Britain: 2000 Edition.* Department of the Environment, Transport and the Regions.

230 FOE, 1999. *ibid*

231 Whitelegg, J., 1993. *Transport for a sustainable future: the case for Europe.* Belhaven Press, London

232 Whitelegg, J., 1993. *ibid*

233 Gover, M. P., 1994. *UK petrol and diesel demand: energy and emission effects of a switch to diesel.* Report for the Department of Trade and Industry, HMSO, London.

234 Vehicle Certification Agency, 2001 at www.vca.gov.

235 Rousseaux, P., C. Hugrel and J. Villien., 1996. *Partial LCA of different means of transport.* Proceedings of the 4th Symposium for case studies, SETAC-Europe, 3 December 1996. Brussels, Belgium.

236 Holman, C. and Fergusson, M., 1992. *Environmental targets for a national transport policy.* in Roberts (ed.) (1992) p18-34.

237 OU, 1993. *Resources and the Environment.* The Open University, Milton Keynes.

238 Lafleche, V. and F. Sachetto, 1995. *Italian high-speed train project: a life cycle comparison of four means of transportation.* EcoBilan Group, Milan, Italy.

239 DETR, 1997. *The Sea Empress Incident: Summary of Report General Introduction.* Department of the Environment, Transport and the Regions. 17th January 1997, HMSO, London.

240 BMLSS, 2001. *Oil Tanker Disasters: Oiled Bird Count.* British Marine Life Study Society, at
http://ourworld.compuserve.com/homepages/BMLSS/oilspil1.htm

241 The Food Commission, 2000. *Veg have lost their minerals.* The Food Magazine, 50th Issue July/September, 2000.

242 Bender and Bender. *Nutrition Reference Handbook.* Oxford University Press 1997

243 Fafunso, M. and Bassir, O. 1976. Effect of cooking on the vitamin C content of fresh leaves and wilted leaves. *J.Agric. Fd. Chemistry.* 24, 354-355

244 MAFF, 1996. *Manual of Nutrition.* The Stationery Office. 10th Edition. 1996

245 Zepplin, M. and Elvehjem, C.A., 1944. Effect of refrigeration on retention of ascorbic acid in vegetables. *Food Research.* 9, 100-111

246 Hunter K.J. and Fletcher J.M. *Effects of processing and storage on the antioxidant activity in vegetables.* Unilever Research, Colworth, n/d unpublished.

247 Hoskins, R., and T. Lobstein, 1999. *How green are our apples? A look at the environmental and social effects of apple production.* The SAFE Alliance, London.

248 *Port Distances.* At http://www.distances.com/

249 H. J. Whiffen and L. B. Bobroff., 1993. *Managing The Energy Cost of Food.* Report EES-99, Florida Cooperative Extension Service, Institute of Food and Agricultural Sciences, University of Florida. May 1993.

250 H. J. Whiffen and L. B. Bobroff., 1993. *ibid*

251 H. J. Whiffen and L. B. Bobroff., 1993. *ibid*

252 UKFG, 2001. *Choosing sustainable agriculture, challenging industrial agriculture.* UK Food Group Conference, Kew Gardens, February 26th 2001.

REFERENCES

253 UKFG, 2001. ibid

254 RAFI, 1997. *Human Nature: Agricultural biodiversity and farm-based food security.* Rural Advancement Foundation International for the FAO. Ottawa, Canada.

255 RAFI, 1997. ibid

256 UNEP, 2001. *Globalisation Threat To World's Cultural, Linguistic And Biological Diversity.* UNEP, Nairobi, 2001.

257 UNEP, 2001. ibid

258 Pretty, J., and Hine, R. 2000. *Feeding the World with Sustainable Agriculture: A Summary of New Evidence.* SAFE-World Research Project, University of Essex.

259 Eurostat, 2000 Statistical Office of the European Community.

260 Eurostat, 2000 Statistical Office of the European Community.

261 Eurostat, 2000 Statistical Office of the European Community.

262 Environmental Health, 2001. *Modern farming methods increase risks.* The Official Journal of the Chartered Institute of Environmental Health, London, 2nd March 2001

263 Environmental Health, 2001. *ibid*

264 Environmental Health, 2001. *ibid*

265 CIWF, 2001. *Action Plan for Reform of Modern Agriculture* Compassion in World Farming, Petersfield, UK, March 2001

266 BBC, 2001. *You and Yours.* BBC Radio 4, April 6th 2001.

267 Caroline Lucas, 2001. *Stopping the Great Food Swap - Relocalising Europe's food supply.* Green Party, 2001

268 FAO statement – www.fao.org/ag/AGA/AGAH/EUFMD/news/2001ukho.htm

269 *Landmark* No 39 March/April 2001

270 *The Daily Telegraph,* 2001. *Pig virus setback for farmers.* The Daily Telegraph 16/8/2001 p4.

271 *Agra Europe,* 2001. Beetle threat to UK potatoes. May 18th 2001.

272 Sean Beer, 2000. *The dynamics of the international supply of beef and sheep meat to the UK.* Nuffield Farming Scholarships Trust, The Centre for Land Based Studies, Bournemouth University, 2000.

273 Sean Beer, 2000. *ibid*

274 Sean Beer, 2000. *ibid*

275 HTV, 2001. *All you can eat.* HTV Wales 9/8/2001.

276 Colin Hines, 2000. *Localisation: a global manifesto.* Earthscan, London.

277 World Development Movement, 2001. *The new rulers of the world.* Carlton Television, Birmingham, UK.

278 World Development Movement, 2001. *The new rulers of the world.* Carlton Television, Birmingham, UK.

279 UNCTAD, 2000. *Least developed countries report 2000.* UNCTAD, New York and Geneva, 2000.

280 John Madeley, 2000, *Hungry for Trade.* Zed Books, London.

281 FAO, 1999. *FAO Symposium on Agriculture, Trade and Food Security.* Geneva, 23-24 September 1999, Synthesis of Case Studies, X3065/E. Rome.

282 H. Barrett et. al., 1999. Globalisation and the changing networks of food supply:the importation of fresh horticultural produce from Kenya into the UK. *Transactions of the Institute of British Geographers* Vol 24 p159-174, British Geographical Society, 1999.

283 H. Barrett et. al., 1999. *ibid*

284 H. Barrett et. al., 1999. *ibid*

285 H. Barrett et. al., 1999. *ibid*

286 H. Barrett et. al., 1999. *ibid*

287 FAO, 2001. *Food Balance Database. 2001.* Food and Agriculture Organisation, Rome at www.fao.org

288 H. Barrett et. al., 1999. *ibid*

289 H. Barrett et. al., 1999. *ibid*

290 FAO, 2001. *Food Balance Database. 2001.* Food and Agriculture Organisation, Rome at www.fao.org

291 World Development Movement, 2001. *The new rulers of the world.* Carlton Television, Birmingham, UK.

292 World Development Movement, 2001. ibid

293 World Development Movement, 2001. ibid

294 World Development Movement, 2001. ibid

295 Meadows, D., 2000.Can Organic Farming Feed the World? *Organic Gardening Magazine,* USA, May 2000

296 FAO, 2000. *The State of Food Insecurity in the World.* Food and Agriculture Organisation, Rome

297 For examples of food poverty in the UK see, for example, Department of Health, (1999) *Saving Lives: Our Healthier Nation: a contract for health.* London: The Stationary Office; and Sustain (2001) *Food Poverty: Policy Options for the New Millennium.* Sustain, London

298 S. Chambron, 2000. *Straightening the Bent World of the Banana.* Published by EFTA.

299 Banana Link, 2001. *Fairtrade Bananas – From Producer to Consumer.* Banana Link, Norwich, UK

300 BCCCA *Industry Facts,* last updated July 1999.

301 *ICCO Quarterly Bulletin of Statistics* Vol 25 (3) 1998/1999

302 ICCO Website at www.icco.org

303 Chris Newell, 2000. TWIN Trading representative, personal communication to the Fairtrade Foundation, January 2000.

REFERENCES

304   Padi, B. and Owusu, G. K., 1998. *Towards an Integrated Pest Management for Sustainable Cocoa Production in Ghana.* Cocoa Research Institute of Ghana, p.11

305   Divine Chocolate Company Website at www. divinechocolate.com

306   *Food Magazine* Oct/Dec 1999, The Food Commission, London.

307   Beth Herzfeld, 2001. Slave Labour. Anti-Slavery International, *Landmark,* May/June 2001 Edition 20. Farmers World Network.

308   Save the Children Fund, 2001. *Child trafficking in West Africa.* Landmark, May/June 2001 Edition 20. Farmers World Network.

309   Save the Children Fund, 2001. *ibid*

310   Divine Chocolate Company Website

311   UK Food Group, 1999. *Bananas: The "Green Gold" of the TNCs* by Anne-Claire Chambron, for the UK Food Group, London

312   UK Food Group, 1999. *ibid*

313   *Background to the banana trade/industry.* Bananalinks.org.uk website

314   *Background to the banana trade/industry.* Bananalinks.org.uk website

315   Don Pollard, 2001. *Costa Rica banana workers face persecution over union membership.* Chair of the RAAW national committee, Landworker, Stoneleigh, UK, May/June 2001.

316   Don Pollard, 2001. *ibid*

317   Don Pollard, 2001. *ibid*

318   Banana Link, 2001.*From Producer to Consumer- Fairtrade Bananas.,* Norwich, UK

319   Banana Link, 2001.ibid

320   Banana Link, 2001.ibid

321   Thilo Bode, 1995. Executive Director of Greenpeace International quoted in a Greenpeace press release on 14th November 1995

322   Jean Damu and David Bacon, 2001.*Oil Rules Nigeria.* Third World Traveller at http://www.thirdworldtraveler.com/Transnational_corps/OilRules_Nigeria.html

323   World Development Movement, 2001. *The new rulers of the world.* Carlton Television, Birmingham, UK.

324   Amnesty International, 2000. *Amnesty International statement on Premier Oil's involvement in Burma.* Press Release, 12th April 2000, Amnesty International, London

325   Michael Ross, 2001. *Extractive sectors and the poor.* Oxfam America

326   World Development Movement, 2001. *The new rulers of the world.* Carlton Television, Birmingham, UK.

327   Chris Hajzler, 2001. *Nigerian Oil Economy: Development or Dependence,* dissertation, Department of Economics, University of Saskatchewan

328   USDOE, 2001. *Nigeria.* Energy Information Administration, Department of the Environment, USA, April 2001, at www.eia.doe.gov

329   USDOE, 2001. *ibid*

330   Jean Damu and David Bacon, 2001. *ibid*

331   Daniel Omoweh, 1998. *Shell and Land Crisis in Rural Nigeria: A Case Study of the Isoko Oil Areas.* Scandinavian Journal of Development Alternatives and Area Studies (Vol. 17), 1998.

332   Chris Hajzler, 2001. *Nigerian Oil Economy: Development or Dependence,* dissertation, Department of Economics, University of Saskatchewan

333   Human Rights Watch, 1999. *The Price of Oil.* Human Rights Watch, New York

334   Daniel Omoweh, 1998. *ibid*

335   Daniel A. Omoweh, 1995. *Shell, Environmental Pollution, and Health in Nigeria.* Afrika Spectrum (vol.30). 1995.

336   World Development Movement, 2001. *The new rulers of the world.* Carlton Television, Birmingham, UK.

337   Daly, H. and Cobb, J., 1990. *For The Common Good.* Green Print: London.

338   Ekins, P., 1989. *Sustainable Consumerism.* New Economics Foundation, London.

339   Nav Brah and Ferd Schelleman, 2000. *Green Purchasing of Foodstuffs.* Swedish Environmental Protection Agency, Stockholm

340   Mollison, B., 1988. *Permaculture: a designers manual.* Tagari: Tyalgum, Australia.

341   Jones, J. A., 1999. *The environmental impacts of distributing consumer goods: a case study on dessert apples.* PhD Thesis (unpublished). Centre for Environmental Strategy, University of Surrey, Guildford, Surrey, UK.

342   A. and J. Gear, 2001. Viewpoint. *The Organic Way,* Issue 163, Spring 2001, Henry Doubleday Research Association

343   The Soil Association, 2001. *The organic food and farming report 2000.* The Soil Association, Bristol

344   The Soil Association, 2001. *ibid*

345   The Soil Association, 2001. *ibid*

346   The Soil Association, 2001. *ibid*

347   The Soil Association, 2001. *ibid*

348   OTB, 2001. *An outline Organic Action Plan,* Organic Targets Bill Streeting Group, Sustain

349   Sustain, 2001. *Outline Organic Action Plan for England and Wales.* Sustain, London, August 2001.

350   The Soil Association, 2001. *ibid*

351   The Soil Association, 2001. *ibid*

352   Cohen NL, Cooley JP, Hall RB, Stoddard AM., 1997. Community supported agriculture: a study of members' dietary patterns and food practices. In: *Agricultural Production and Nutrition,* School of Nutrition, Tufts University, USA

REFERENCES

[353] Carlisle D., 2001. *Great Oaks from little acorns grow*. Health Development Today 2001;4:20-23.

[354] Pretty, 2001. *Taking Back the Middle for Farmers and Communities*. At www.essex.ac.uk/ces

[355] Anna Ross, 2001. *How Much Is That Carrot in the Window? Supermarkets' claims of low organic food prices are misleading*. Senior Lecturer in Economics at the University of the West of England, Bristol

[356] Anna Ross, 2001. *ibid*

[357] MAFF, 2000. *Basic horticultural statistics for the UK*, Calendar years 1989/90 –1999-00 MAFF, HMSO,

[358] Pretty, J. N., 1995. *Regenerating Agriculture: Policies and Practice for Sustainability and Self-Reliance*. Earthscan, London.

[359] see www.localfood.org.uk and *Growing Food in Cities*. Garnett, T. (1996) National Food Alliance/SAFE Alliance (now Sustain), London.

[360] Local food schemes also include Urban Agriculture. For more information see the websites of Sustain at www.sustainweb.org; The Foundation for Local Food Initiatives at www.localfood.org.uk and the Food Futures and Local Food Links programmes run by the Soil Association at www.soilassociation.org.uk.

[361] Jules Pretty, 1998. *Sustainable Development for Local Economies*. Centre for Environment and Society, University of Essex, September 1998 at http://www2.essex.ac.uk/ces/ResearchProgrammes/loceconsd.htm

[362] BBC, 2001. *Changing Places*. BBC Radio 4, 24/9/2001.

[363] WyeCycle, 2000. *Memorandum by WyeCycle (DSW 05)*. Submission to the Select Committee on Environment, Transport and Regional Affairs, September 2000 at http://www.parliament.the-stationery-office.co.uk/pa/cm199900/cmselect/cmenvtra/903/903m06.htm

[364] Julian Rose, 1998. Countryside, What Countryside? *Permaculture Magazine* No. 23, Permaculture Association.

[365] Caroline Lucas, 2001. *Stopping the Great Food Swap - Relocalising Europe's food supply*. Green Party, 2001

[366] FAO, 2001. *Food Balance Database*. *2001*. Food and Agriculture Organisation, Rome at www.fao.org

[367] Swedish Environmental Protection Agency, 1999. *A sustainable food supply chain*. Report 4966. SEPA: Stockholm.

[368] Data for shipping and airfreight from *Guidelines for company reporting on greenhouse gas emissions*. Department of the Environment, Transport and the Regions: London, March 2001. Data for trucks is based on Whitelegg, J., 1993. *Transport for a sustainable future: the case for Europe*. Belhaven Press, London; and Gover, M. P., 1994. *UK petrol and diesel demand: energy and emission effects of a switch to diesel*. Report for the Department of Trade and Industry, HMSO, London. Data for cars from the Vehicle Certification Agency at www.vca.gov.uk; Whitelegg, J., 1993. *Transport for a sustainable future: the case for Europe*. Belhaven Press, London; and Gover, M. P., 1994. *UK petrol and diesel demand: energy and emission effects of a switch to diesel*. Report for the Department of Trade and Industry, HMSO, London.

[369] Caroline Hill, 2001. *Local food better for rural economy than supermarket shopping*. News Release, New Economics Foundation, August 2001.

[370] Charles Couzens, Emma Delow and Sarah Watson, 2000. *Local Food Links in the South West of England*. f3 - The Foundation for Local Food Initiatives, Bristol, UK

[371] Nick Robins and Sarah Roberts, 1998. *Consumption in a Sustainable World*, Background paper for a Workshop, June 2-4, 1998, Kabelvaag, Norway. International Institute for Environment and Development on behalf of the Ministry of the Environment, Norway

[372] *Elm Farm Newsletter*, 2001. Elm Farm Research Centre, March 2001

[373] IATP, 2000. *Cultivating Havana: Urban Agriculture and Food Security in the Years of Crisis*. Institute for Food and Development Policy/Food First. Oakland, CA, 2000.

[374] Renee Kjartan, 2000. *Castro Topples Pesticide in Cuba*. Washington Free Press, August 7, 2000

[375] Renee Kjartan, 2000. *ibid*

[376] Renee Kjartan, 2000. *ibid*

[377] IATP, 2000. *Cultivating Havana: Urban Agriculture and Food Security in the Years of Crisis*. Institute for Food and Development Policy/Food First. Oakland, CA, 2000.

[378] Quoted in *Countryside, What Countryside?* Julian Rose, Permaculture Magazine No. 23

[379] DEFRA, 2001. *A new department a new agenda: Aims and Objectives – have your say*. DEFRA Consultation Document, Department of the Environment, Food and Rural Affairs, 2001

[380] DEFRA, 2001. *Policy Commission on Farming and Food - Terms of reference*. Department of the Environment, Food and Rural Affairs, 2001, at www.defra.gov.uk

[381] DEFRA, 2001. *ibid*

[382] see, for example, *The new protectionism: protecting the future against free trade*. Tim Lang and Colin Hines, Earthscan, 1993; *Localisation: a global manifesto*. Colin Hines, Earthscan, 2000; Caroline Lucas, 2001. *Stopping the Great Food Swap - Relocalising Europe's food supply*. Green Party, 2001; *Regenerating Agriculture: Policies and practice for sustainability and self-reliance*. Pretty, J. N. 1995, Earthscan, London. Böge, S. (1993) *Road Transport of Goods and the Effects on the Spatial Environment*. Wupperthal University; Paxton, A. (1994) *The Food Miles Report: The Dangers of Long Distance Food Transport*. The SAFE Alliance, London.

[383] DEFRA, 2001. *A new department a new agenda: Aims and Objectives – have your say*. DEFRA Consultation Document, Department of the Environment, Food and Rural Affairs, 2001

[384] *ENDS Environment Daily*, EU sustainability indicators proposed. Issue 1093 Wednesday 31st October 2001.

[385] *ENDS Environment Daily*, EU sustainability plan heading for a fall. Issue 1010 Friday 15th June 2001.

[386] *ENDS Environment Daily*, EU sustainable development strategy adopted. Issue 1011 Monday 18th June 2001

[387] ENDS Environment Daily, *EU sustainable development strategy adopted*. Issue 1011 Monday 18th June 2001

REFERENCES

388   Sustain, 2001. *Local food sourcing – PR or the real thing?* (unpublished report), A survey by Sustain, April 2001

389   Pippa Gallop, 2001. The great local food scam. *Corporate Watch Newsletter*, May-June 2001.

390   FSA, 2001. *Consumer attitudes to food standards.* Final Report, Prepared for the Food Standards Agency and COI Communications by RSGB, January 2001.

391   The concept of a 'pollution factor' originates from - Breach, J., 1998. *Pollution by Supermarkets.* Letter sent all Members of Parliament on 29 July 1998 by John Breach, Tonbridge, Kent, and Breach, J. (1998) *Pollution by Supermarkets/Regulation of Major Multiple Retailers.* Letter sent all Members of Parliament on 9 November 1998 by John Breach, Tonbridge, Kent.

392   VTPI, 2001. *Freight Management: Reducing Commercial Vehicle Traffic.* TDM Encyclopedia, Victoria Transport Policy Institute, Victoria, Canada at www.vtpi.org

393   DETR, 1999. *Sustainable Distribution: A Strategy.* Department of the Environment, Transport and the Regions (www.roads.detr.gov.uk), 1999.

394   VTPI, 2001. *ibid*

395   DETR, 1999. *ibid*

396   DETR, 1999. *ibid*

397   RCEP, 1994. *Transport and the Environment* 18th Report of the Royal Commission on Environmental Pollution, HMSO, London.

398   Forum for the Future, 2001. Blair speech offset by budget compromise. *Green Futures* May/June 2001, Forum for the Future, London

399   See for example: *Promoting Local Food in Oxfordshire.* Kate de Selincourt and Charles Couzens, Oxfordshire County Council, 2001; and *Local Food Links in the South West of England.* Charles Couzens, Emma Delow and Sarah Watson, f3 - The Foundation for Local Food Initiatives, Bristol, UK, November 2000.

400   Sustain, 2001. *Draft action plan for England and Wales – a discussion document.* The organic food and farming targets bill campaign, Sustain, 2001.

401   Shrybman, S., 1999. *A citizen's guide to the world trade organisation.* Canadian Centre for Policy Alternatives, Ottawa

Contacts List

Centre for Alternative Technology - www.cat.org.uk
Centre for Environment and Society - www.essex.ac.uk/ces
Centre for Food Policy - www.foodpolicy.co.uk
Common Ground - www.commonground.org.uk
Compassion in World Farming - www.ciwf.co.uk
Council for the Protection of Rural England - www.cpre.org.uk
Countryside Agency - www.countryside.gov.uk
Department for Environment, Food and Rural Affairs - www.defra.gov.uk
East Anglia Food Link - www.eafl.org.uk
Ecologist - www.thecologist.org
Elm Farm Research Centre - www.efrc.com
Federation of City Farms and Community Gardens - www.farmgarden.org.uk
Five Year Freeze - www.fiveyearfreeze.org
Food Commission - www.foodcomm.org.uk
Food From Britain - www.foodfrombritain.com
Food Standards Agency - www.foodstandards.gov.uk
Foundation for Local Food Initiatives - www.localfood.org.uk
Friends of the Earth - www.foe.co.uk
Gaia Foundation - www.gaianet.org
Genetics Forum - www.geneticsforum.org.uk
Guild of Food Writers - www.gfw.co.uk
Henry Doubleday Research Association - www.hdra.org.uk
Institute for European Environmental Policy - www.ieep.org.uk
Institute of Agriculture and Trade Policy - www.iatp.org
Intergovernmental Panel on Climate Change - www.ipcc.ch
Intermediate Technology - www.oneworld.org/itdg
International Society for Ecology and Culture - www.isec.org.uk
London Farmers Markets - www.londonfarmersmarkets.com
National Farmers Union - www.nfu.org.uk
National Consumer Council - www.ncc.org.uk
National Federation of Farmers Markets - www.farmersmarkets.net
National Federation of Women's Institutes - www.nfwi.org.uk
New Economics Foundation - www.neweconomics.org
Permaculture Association - www.permaculture.org.uk
Pesticides Action Network - www.pan-uk.org
PlantLife - www.plantlife.org.uk
Royal Society for the Protection of Birds - www.rspb.org.uk
Rural Agricultural and Allied Workers (TGWU) - www.tgwu.org.uk
Soil Association - www.soilassociation.org
Somerset Food Links - www.somerset.foodlinks.org.uk
Stockholm Environment Institute - www.seiy.org
Sustain - www.sustainweb.org
UK Food Group - www.ukfg.org.uk
Women's Environmental Network - www.gn.apc.org/wen
World Transport Policy and Practice - www.ecoplan.org/wtpp
WWF-UK - www.wwf-uk.org
Worldwatch Institute - www.worldwatch.org
Wyecycle - www.wye.org.uk/business/directory/wyecycle.htm